Copyright © 2019 by Simon Mansfield

All rights reserved. No part of this book may be reproduced or used in any manner without written permission of the copyright owner except for the use of quotations in a book review. For more information, address:
simon_mansfield@rocketmail.com

FIRST EDITION

www.evergreenbusinessdevelopment.co.uk
simon@evergreenbusinessdevelopment.co.uk

Contents

HOW TO WRITE A BUSINESS PLAN — 4

Introduction — 4

Deciding to start a business and managing risk — 8

From paid employment to running a business — 12

How to trade, self-employment or Ltd company — 16

Setting a financial personal plan — 18

Business plan – the basics — 23

Tips for generating high sales — 25

Tips for reducing cost — 28

Self-employed business model — 30

Alternative business model (increased income) — 31

Tax efficiency — 35

WRITING A BUSINESS PLAN — 40

Executive Summary (800 – 1,000 words) — 44

Products and Services (800 – 1,000 words) — 46

Marketing and Lead Generation (1,000 – 1,600 words) — 50

Competitor Analysis (300 – 400 words) — 53

Company Structure (600 – 1,000 words) — 54

SWOT Analysis (100 – 200 words) — 58

Financial Analysis (400 – 800 words)	60
CHLOE'S CHOCOLATES LTD (BUSINESS PLAN)	**66**
Executive Summary	67
Products and Services	72
Marketing and Lead Generation	76
Competitor Analysis	84
Company Structure	87
SWOT Analysis	93
Financial Analysis	94
MICHELLE HEART LIFE COACHING LTD (BUSINESS PLAN)	**97**
Executive Summary	98
Products and Services	104
Marketing and Lead Generation	112
Competitor Analysis	122
Company Structure	123
SWOT Analysis	128
Financial Analysis	129

How to Write a Business Plan

(Your Guide to Starting a Business)

Introduction

If you only do what you can, you will never be more than you are. Not sure who first said this, but continuous self-improvement and pushing personal boundaries are valuable qualities needed to become an entrepreneur. Many people dream of starting their first business and being their own boss, but are put off for several reasons:

1. Fear of the unknown
2. Consider it to be too difficult
3. Love the dreaming but can't follow anything through
4. Unable to obtain the necessary business skills or qualifications
5. Fear of failure
6. **Not knowing where to start**

Writing a business plan is the perfect place to start. A business plan acts as a blue-print, a document to guide the directors and be referenced as the business expands. The plan should be reviewed and updated regularly to ensure it remains relevant.

Starting a business is a big step for most entrepreneurs and should be approached in the same way as any large project. breaking activities into smaller tasks and capturing ideas in a document will make starting a business more manageable. This How-to Guide will help you through the process of writing a business plan. Create your vision of what you want your business to do, how you want to delivery it and some of the practical steps that sometimes get overlooked.

Example; The threshold for VAT registration for 2019/20 is £85,000 in a rolling 12-month period. I have known several business owners get caught out thinking the threshold is per financial year resulting in a costly mistake.

I have been writing business plans for over 20 years for large corporations, small company start-ups and the National Health Service (NHS). The NHS is arguably one of the most challenging business environments. I have seen first-hand the positive effect of business planning and the negative side of failing to plan properly. A business plan is a tool to enable ideas to be tested. Marketing can be researched and documented to ensure target markets are reached in an effective way. Pricing will be calculated and benchmarked against competitors. Identifying the optimum price for a product or service will maximum sales. Often new businesses price their products or services too low which can lead to a lot of work, for little financial return. Setting a price too high may result in no sales at all.

Personally, I am deeply passionate to provide everyone with access to good affordable information before starting their business. Therefore, I wrote this How-to Guide. I have provided two sample business plans. One for a product-based business selling through multiple channels. The second business is service-based.

In 2011 I made a mistake when I started my own business, Evergreen Accountancy Ltd. I thought I knew what my business would be. After a few months 80% of my time was directed to writing business plans and soon realised my company should have been called something different. I had specialised writing financial business plans instead of providing financial accounting services. It is ok to make mistakes in business, learning from them is part of the cycle of improvement that often leads to a greater positive outcome.

For most of my career I have been employed by organisations with a strong sense of identify that are values driven. During my 20 years at The Body Shop Int PLC I learnt to combine the need to deliver company profit with delivering corporate ethical values. Ethical values were used as marketing to deliver profit. Greater profit lead to further ethical value projects. The cycle continued this way for several decades. The Body Shop was founded in 1976 and is best known for its "against animal testing campaign", something that resonated with its customers. The UK consumer was no longer prepared to tolerate cosmetic products tested on animals. The Body Shop founder Anita Roddick considered her corporate values from the outset and rigorously stuck to them by embedding them within the workforce and culture. The Body Shop was sold to L'Oréal in 2006 for £652.3m.

Other companies demonstrate corporate values in different ways, they may:

1. Set up charity foundations that support and run alongside their business.
2. Have a policy to support the community and actively engage in local events.
3. Donate money to local charities through collection boxes.
4. Have a policy to support staff, introducing incentives.

Example; A business may have a strong value of fairness to employees. What does this really mean? Firstly, a company will need to explain their values either in a policy document, a mission statement or strapline. This will show customers what the business stands for and is committed to achieving. It also means the business will live by these values and consider them in all the decision making. A company might commit to:

1. Paying all employees, a living wage or at least 10% higher than similar roles locally? Whichever is the highest.
2. Commitment to equal pay.

3. Commitment to provide a good pension above the national minimum standard.
4. Annual appraisals and ongoing personal development for everyone.

The benefits to the business:

1. The company may attract a high standard of applicants. When jobs become vacant a higher quality workforce can be employed.
2. Branding and customer awareness may increase. Customers regard companies who look after their staff well as a comparison to how they will look after them.

Company directors can define the corporate values and create a brand around them that are considered most important and relevant. They tell customers about them in an engaging way, allowing them to feel part of the brand that will inspire loyalty. This will add value to a product or service and provide a strategic advantage over competitors.

Deciding to start a business and managing risk

Running a business requires self-motivation and for some people this can be difficult. Self-employment or directorship is not for everyone. Business owners I have spoken to often talk about the start-up phase as being disorderly, complicated, sometimes chaotic and stressful. The same people also describe it as exciting, rewarding and the best time of their life. Some people thrive in situations like this, while for others this can feel daunting and overwhelming.

The health of a business is usually defined by financial and quality measures. Financial measures are defined by sales, profit or assets. Quality measures might include customer satisfaction or the number of complaints.

For entrepreneurs starting a business, similar considerations apply to personal health and wellbeing. How will your finances change when you start your business? How will starting a business affect your quality of life? Personal quality might include happiness, enjoyment or fulfilment.

1. Are you currently happy?
2. How will starting a business affect how happy you are?
3. Do you know what is involved?
4. How much time will it take?
5. Are you currently financially secure?
6. How will this change if you start a business?

Choosing to be happy?

Many people think about starting their own business but are put off because they see difficulties ahead. A lack of self-confidence or wage uncertainty. Sometimes taking a risk is simply, too risky.

Risks can be mitigated, either in part or completely. There are many risk management tools available, but simply, mitigating risk comes down to the following:

1. Identifying the nature of each risk.
2. Assessing how likely and severe each risk is.
3. Create a list of actions to mitigate each risk.
4. Assess the impact of your mitigation. Will the actions completely remove the risk, reduce it or can you tolerate the risk?

By scoring each risk out of 5 in both likelihood and consequence and multiplying the numbers will create a risk score. The risk score will determine the risk level.

		CONSEQUENCE				
		Insignificant	Minor	Moderate	Major	Catastrophic
LIKELIHOOD	Almost Certain	5	10	15	20	25
	Likely	4	8	12	16	20
	Possible	3	6	9	12	15
	Unlikely	2	4	6	8	10
	Rare	1	2	3	4	5

	Overall Score
Extreme	15 and over
High	9 to 14
Medium	5 to 8
Low	4 and less

The table below shows how this might be achieved. Take some time to think about obstacles to your success. What worries or concerns do you have? What keeps you awake at night? Make a list of all the risks you can think of and score them using the tables above.

Consequence from insignificant (1) through to catastrophic (5). Likelihood from rare (1) through to almost certain (5).

Next, think about mitigating actions. By listing several mitigating actions (sometimes called countermeasures) a picture can emerge showing how each risk can be addressed.

How do you feel now? You have thought about the risks and listed actions to deal with them. What impact do you think your actions will have? What score would you give your risks after your mitigating actions?

This process is often intuitive rather than analytical. Identifying risks and mitigating actions is one way to help with the transition to become an entrepreneur.

Example; Personal and financial risks might look like this:

Nature of risk	Likelihood of risk (1 to 5)	Severity of risk (1 to 5)	Risk Level	Mitigation of risk	Impact	New Risk Level
Personal – There is a risk that my work will not be good enough, I lack confidence in my abilities that may result in customers being disappointed.	3	4	12	1 - I will start a business in a business sector I know well. 2 - I will secure the services of a mentor and ask them questions I am unsure of. 3 - I will write a business plan to act as a road-map to my success.	75%	3
Financial – There is a risk that I won't be able to earn enough to support my lifestyle and will not be able to provide for my family.	3	5	15	1 – I will be prepared to work longer in the first 12 months to build up a client base. 2 – I will be prepared to claim working and child tax credits in the first year to support my income. 3 – I will supplement my income in year 1 by taking on agency paid work if necessary.	75%	3.75

From paid employment to running a business

Being in paid employment can be an obstacle to starting a business. Many entrepreneurs I have spoken to spent up to two years deciding whether to start their business. Job security can be a difficult thing to give up.

Some entrepreneurs think about starting a business in the same sector as their employment. Others look for a change of industry altogether. Consider the importance of each personal value and how the value relates to your current job and your business venture:

Score the 18 questions (1-5) on importance and then multiply your score (1-5) for each question relating to your current job and new business venture:

Personal Value	Description	Import-ance (1 to 5)	Current job (1 to 5)	Current job score	New business (1 to 5)	New business score
Friendship	To work with people, I respect and to be respected by them.			0		0
Location	To be able to live where I want to live.			0		0
Enjoyment	To enjoy my work. To have fun doing it.			0		0

Personal Value	Description	Import-ance (1 to 5)	Current job (1 to 5)	Current job score	New business (1 to 5)	New business score
Family	To have time with my family. Good work life balance.			0		0
Leadership	To motivate and energize other people.			0		0
Personal Development	To learn and to do challenging work that will help me develop.			0		0
Security	To have a steady income that fully meets my family's needs.			0		0
Wisdom	To grow in understanding of myself, my personal calling and life's real purpose.			0		0
Community	To be deeply involved with a group that has a larger purpose beyond one's self.			0		0

Personal Value	Description	Import-ance (1 to 5)	Current job (1 to 5)	Current job score	New business (1 to 5)	New business score
Wealth	To earn a great deal of money (i.e., well beyond my family's basic needs). To be financially independent.			0		0
Expertness	To become a known and respected authority in what I do.			0		0
Service	To contribute to the well being and satisfaction of others. To help people who need help and improve society.			0		0
Prestige	To be seen by others as successful. To become well known. To obtain recognition and status in my chosen field.			0		0

Personal Value	Description	Import-ance (1 to 5)	Current job (1 to 5)	Current job score	New business (1 to 5)	New business score
Power	To have the authority to approve or disapprove proposed courses of action. To make assignments and control allocation of people and resources.			0		0
Independence	To have freedom of thought and action. To be able to act in terms of my own time schedules and priorities.			0		0
Integrity	To live and work in compliance with my personal moral standards. To be honest and acknowledge/stand up for my personal beliefs.			0		0
Health	To be physically and mentally fit.			0		0
Creativity	To be innovative. To create new and better ways of doing things.			0		0
				0		0

The total score may help you with your decision to start a business.

How to trade, self-employment or Ltd company

Most people choose to trade either as a sole trader or a Ltd company. There are other structures, including partnerships or community interest companies, but most business owners trade in one of these two ways.

Typically, sole traders or self-employed people trade as individuals and are often smaller businesses. Ltd companies are typically larger and employ people. This is not always the case; sole traders can employ other people and limited companies can involve an individual.

There are other important factors to consider:

Sole trader /self-employment – The main advantage is simplicity, owners can begin trading just by notifying HMRC. Your tax liability can be aligned to the financial year and accounting costs are usually lower. Often sole traders save on banking fees because their business bank account can be in their name rather than the business name, benefiting from free banking.

Tax liability is variable depending on individual circumstances. As rule of thumb a business trading as a sole trader will pay on average 2%-4% more tax than a Ltd company. This is mainly because a limited company has more options to extract money including payments to directors as dividends. While 4% does not sound much, consider a business with £50,000 profit before tax, 4% equates to £2,000.

Limited companies – There are two main advantages of trading as a limited company. Firstly, directors are likely to pay less personal tax. This is because shareholders can take a small salary and draw other income in the form of dividends. Secondly the business is a distinct entity separate from the business owner. This means the business owner is not financially liable for any loss made by the business giving them additional protection.

Before trading - Compare your likely tax liability between a Ltd Company and sole trader online using several available tools. All good search engines will show on-line calculators simply by searching sole trader v Ltd company calculator. Be aware of this before trading and registering your business with Companies House and HMRC (for Ltd companies) or just HMRC for self-employment.

Once Trading - Consider checking your tax liability a few months before your year-end to assess your tax liability. This will give an idea of how much tax will need to be set aside. Some businesses vary their investment towards the end of a financial year. This may enable company profit and director's income to fall under corporation tax and personal income tax thresholds.

Setting a financial personal plan

Setting a financial personal plan will calculate how much money is needed to support the business owner's lifestyle.

Calculating how much money is needed is done by making a list of all personal expenditure. Look at old bank and credit card statements to provide actual outgoings. This will be more accurate than estimating. Include everything, particularly expensive items such as a car purchase, summer holiday and Christmas. Infrequent large purchases can be overlooked.

Example; The tables below are based on a couple, Mr and Mrs Heart with one small child who have decided the following:

1. Mrs Heart wants to start her own life coaching business. After a successful career in Human Resources, Mrs Heart has decided to work for herself and is motivated to provide services to as many people as possible.
2. Mrs Heart will reduce her income in the first year as her business will not be fully established. She is concerned about not having enough money to support her family.
3. Mr Heart will continue to work as a car mechanic earning £10 per hour.
4. They want to earn enough to support their lifestyle. They will replace their car every few years and go on holiday each summer.
5. Gross, and net income has been calculated based on the 2019/20 tax year.
6. Expenditure has been calculated using old bank statements to be as accurate as possible.
7. Both Mr and Mrs Heart will utilise their income tax free allowance. There is no need to transfer 10% income tax allowance. Both incomes meet or exceed the income tax threshold. Transferring 10% tax free allowance to a spouse is

achieved by a call to HMRC. A confirmation letter is issued a few days later.
8. No other jobs or income are planned. Mr Smith may be offered overtime, but this is not guaranteed and has not been factored into the plan.

Gross Income

	Monthly Gross Income (£)	Annual Gross Income (£)	Annual National insurance (£)	Annual Gross Income Tax (£)	Annual Net Income (£)
Mr Heart	1,421	19,875	-1,349	-1475	17,051
Mrs Heart	1,003	12,500	-464	0	12,036
Total Income	2,424	32,375	-1,813	-1475	29,087

Net Income

	Monthly Net Income (£)	Annual Net Income (£)
Main job / self-employment income	2,424	29,087
Other job part /full time	0	0
Benefits	0	0
Use of personal savings	0	0
Other Income	0	0
Total Income	2,424	29,087

Expenditure	Monthly Net Income (£)	Annual Net Income (£)
Rent / Mortgage interest 1)	500	6,000
Mortgage capital repayments 1)	0	0
Personal loan(s) Repayments 4)	0	0
Council tax	150	1,800
Electricity / gas	110	1,320
Water	30	360
Mobile phone/s	60	720
Broadband	30	360
TV License	13	156
Personal and Property Insurance	40	480
Entertainment and Holidays 2)	120	1,440
Subscriptions e.g. Gym	0	0
Food	350	4,200
Clothing	200	2,400
Car tax & insurance	25	300
Car running expenses (inc fuel)	200	2,400
Contingency	100	1,200
Money put into savings 4)	0	0
Children Expenditure	200	2,400
Car depreciation or loan costs 2)	167	2,004
Christmas 3)	100	1,200
Total Expenditure	2,395	28,740
Total Surplus or Deficit 5)	**29**	**347**

1) Reducing mortgage payments to interest only will enable the family to continue with their lifestyle. When Mrs Hearts income increases as her business develops, capital repayments will be made.
2) Large expenditure items such as replacing the family car every few years and having an annual holiday is part of the plan. Money will be put away each month.
3) Christmas is an annual expense and will be funded by putting away £100 each month.
4) The family has £2,000 savings as a contingency fund. This is over and above any money set aside for holidays, cars and Christmas. Savings over the next year will be maintained. No further loans will be taken out in the next 12 months.
5) Mr and Mrs Heart are planning a small surplus in the next 12 months of £347.

Business plan – the basics

Whether you are looking to start a business slowly with no or little start-up capital or wishing to start a business through a loan or an investor, the same business plan principles apply. There are 3 essential criteria that all good business plans must demonstrate:

1. **Good Idea** - Does the business plan have a clear idea and set of objectives? Is it credible and will it deliver with good leadership?
2. **Good Leadership** - Is the business plan deliverable by the owners? What relevant qualifications or experience do they have?
3. **Good Finances** - Do the finances add up? Are the costs and sales expectations realistic?

If you are presenting your idea to an investor or a bank manager and they reject your idea, don't panic. It is important to listen to others and accept their feedback. If one investor rejects your application, there will be others. If you believe in your idea and your capabilities to deliver your plan, move to the next investor. If you don't believe you can make your idea work, then perhaps you should not get started in the first place.

Your start-up financial forecast should be as accurate as possible, and budget for a small contingency. Your contingency should cover:

1. Unexpected item costs.
2. Cover the cost of items where the original budget was insufficient.
3. Cover business losses or cash-flow deficits in the first few months of trading.

Your business plan is primarily for you. What do you want your business to do for you? Of course, you want it to provide an income. How much money do you need or want? How many hours do you have to dedicated to your business?

Some entrepreneurs will be completely focused, have high energy levels and think of very little in their life other than starting a business. Others may have personal time commitments elsewhere, a new or young family or they may need to care for an elderly relative. Consider your time commitment and ambition and factor this into your business from the outset to avoid disappointment later.

Whatever your ambition or time commitment, most business owners aspire to generate high profit in the shortest amount of time:

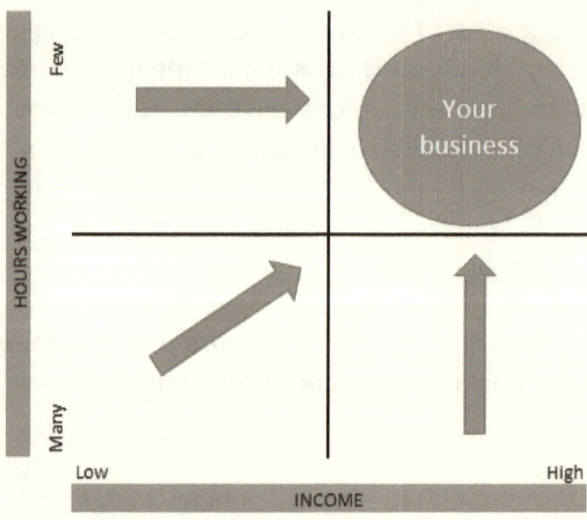

Tips for generating high sales

Generating high sales is achieved either through high unit sales, a high price point or both. Developing an optimum pricing model will help achieve the two.

Create an optimum selling price – When a business launches a new product the selling price is a key part of the financial business plan and calculated in two ways. Firstly, from the bottom up considering all the individual costs of the product or service:

1. Individual component costs.
2. Labour costs.
3. Delivery costs.
4. Overheads.
5. Profit.

Secondly from a benchmarking approach, looking at similar or equivalent products or services offered by competitors. This will include comparing quality, added value and product performance. Limited competition and new innovative products also command a higher selling price.

Example; A fully qualified ex-Olympian runner considers offering a personal training service to customers across London. The athlete has added value over competitors. This is due to the recognition of achievements/personal success and is regardless of whether client outcomes are better or not.

Setting a price too high compared to the preserved market value is likely to lead to lower sales. Setting the price too low may generate sales at the expense of margin and profit.

Businesses will focus on sales targets and set a recommended retail price (RRP) slightly higher than what they expect to achieve on average. The most important measure is average units at retail (AUR). This will allow for discounts, stock returns, damages and theft.

Example; The table below shows how a retailer who has bought 1,000 units of Bluetooth speakers at £4 each achieves an AUR sales price of £9 per unit:

Purchases		Units	Unit £	Total cost
Purchased		1,000	£4.00	£4,000

Sales	% sold	Units	Unit £	Total sold
Sales (RRP)	85%	850	£10.00	£8,500
Sales (30% promotion)	5%	50	£7.00	£350
Sales (70% promotion)	5%	50	£3.00	£150
Sales (returns)	2%	20	£0.00	£0
Sales (theft)	2%	20	£0.00	£0
Sales (damages)	1%	10	£0.00	£0
Average unit at Retail (AUR)	100%	1,000	£9.00	£9,000

The retailer plans to sell 85% of stock at £10 each, a further 10% is sold at a discount and a further 5% is allocated to stock returns, theft and damaged goods. With these factors the retailer achieves on average £9 per unit.

Good product/service satisfaction – The definition of a good product will mean different things to different customers. Understanding your target market and selling to them is likely to increase satisfaction rates.

Example; Selling a chocolate containing brazil nuts to a customer that does not like the taste of nuts will lead to a disappointment.

Clarity at the point of sale will give customers an informed choice to buy a product. Communication between the business and customers may be through packaging/labelling or a sales conversation. Matching a product to customers' needs in the following areas usually leads to higher product satisfaction:

- Function.
- Reliability.
- Durability.
- Simplicity / ease of use.
- Quality.
- Cost.
- Aesthetics.

Good customer service – will develop into brand loyalty, creating a service that will encourage customers to return and tell their friends. Every company will have a different approach and meaning of good service depending on customer expectations.

Example; A fast-food restaurant may consider speed of service and good food quality as the important contributors to achieving good customer service. Customers at a table service restaurant may expect a different type of customer service. This may include higher quality food and presentation or dedicated staff to achieve an eating experience rather than providing food. Good staff manners and cleanliness would be expected by both restaurants.

Delivering good marketing – Good marketing and communication will enable customers to find your products or services. Having a positive marketing strategy delivered in effective programmes of work to your target market will drive customers to you.

Tips for reducing cost

Businesses use different methods to reduce costs, some focus on automation through IT software. Others might introduce equipment that can make a product quicker and more consistently than a traditional workforce. Some companies may reduce costs through negotiation and contract management with suppliers. Others will look to remove tasks of limited value and reduce waist.

Effective businesses will do all of these and be constantly looking for opportunities to increase margin and profit.

Introduce automation – Successful businesses will review their processes, to identify tasks that are carried out on a regular basis that could be streamlined. Technology or equipment may be introduced to increase productivity and quality.

Process mapping is a helpful way to identify wasteful activities and tasks. Illustrations will allow the presentation of a process to be displayed in a simple way. The process is broken down into individual elements making it easier to understand and visual. Businesses are looking to unlock bottlenecks or "pause points" that slow processes down and identify tasks that are interdependent on others.

Actively seek out waste in all areas. Even large and well managed organisations look to reduce costs by reducing waste. Companies can identify areas with poor value either from direct financial costs or through improving efficiency.

Poor value direct financial cost is usually the result of businesses failing to carry out regular value for money assessments. Examples include cost of premises, staff budgets and component costs.

Example; A product developed and costed 5 years ago will have very different component costs today. Failure to carry out value for money assessments regularly will almost certainly result in reduced profit. If the component cost has increased significantly during this time, it is almost certain that the supplier will make an approach to increase the product cost.

Unless a value for money assessment is carried out regularly, a reduction in component cost will not be identified resulting in a missed opportunity.

Examples of reducing inefficiency include: Staff time waisted at meetings, excessive activity of non-value-added activities. Inefficient time spent replying to emails, constant dealing with unplanned urgent tasks rather than planning effectively. Urgent tasks almost always cost more.

Self-employed business model

If your happy working for yourself, don't want the hassle of managing staff and want a flexible lifestyle then being self-employed might be a good option. The downside is that income can be limited as the owner is solely responsible for generating income.

Example; A high qualified accountant may command £50 per hour for services and realistic to generate customers to an average of 30 chargeable hours per week. The example below shows how a self-employed professional can earn over £50,000 per year:

Self-employed	Hour	Week	Month	Year
Director (income)	£50	£1,500	£6,000	£66,000
Cost of sales	-£2	-£60	-£240	-£2,640
Overheads	-£8	-£240	-£960	-£10,560
Profit (net)	£40	£1,200	£4,800	£52,800

Assumptions:

1. Chargeable hours of £50 per hour.
2. Working on average 30hrs per week chargeable hours, and 7.5hrs on other tasks including lead generation.
3. Work 4 weeks per month.
4. Work 11 months per year.
5. Cost assumptions of 20% to cover cost of sales and overheads.
6. Total income before personal tax is £52,800.

Alternative business model (increased income)

For some people who start a business, the only thing that matters is success. Having a small ambitious business may mean working longer hours, particularly in the start-up phase. To increase income the director will need to identify ways to increase sales. The three most common ways are:

1. **Process automation** – An example might be a retail website that collects orders through software and system interfaces. A third party will collect orders and ship products to customers with no or limited intervention.
2. **Hiring staff** – Staff are employed and work to earn the business owner an additional income. The business owner can generate higher income and accepts the risk of employment that can lead to losses.
3. **Innovation** – An example might be a new product that is first to market, improved design or functionality that people want or need.

Consider the accountancy service business described in the previous chapter. A director's income can be significantly increased if the company employs a workforce:

Self-employed	Hour	Week	Month	Year
Director	£50	£375	£1,500	£16,500
Employee 1	£50	£1,500	£6,000	£66,000
Employee 2	£50	£1,500	£6,000	£66,000
Employee 3	£50	£1,500	£6,000	£66,000
Employee 4	£50	£1,500	£6,000	£66,000
Employee 5	£50	£1,500	£6,000	£66,000
Employee 6	£50	£1,500	£6,000	£66,000
Employee 7	£50	£1,500	£6,000	£66,000
Employee 8	£50	£1,500	£6,000	£66,000
Sales (income)	£450	£12,375	£49,500	£544,500
Cost of sales	-£18	-£540	-£2,160	-£23,760
Overheads	-£72	-£2,160	-£8,640	-£95,040
premises	-£10	-£300	-£1,200	-£13,200
Wages	-£200	-£6,000	-£24,000	-£264,000
Profit (net)	£150	£3,375	£13,500	£148,500

In this example the director's income has increase to £148,500. This is because of the contribution of each employee adding just under £12,000 each to the director's income.

Assumptions:

1. Chargeable hours of £50 per hour.
2. Director has reduced chargeable hours to 1 day per week (more time spend on marketing and team leadership).
3. 8 Employees working on average 30hrs per week chargeable hours, with 4- or 5-weeks holiday per year.
4. Cost assumptions of 20% to cover cost of sales and overheads.
5. Fixed premise costs of £13,200.
6. Wages of the 8 employees including employers NI contribution and pension of £264k per year.

7. Total income before corporation tax is £148,500 (£95,700 more than a self-employed model).
8. Each employee contributes on average £11,963 to the company profit.

The additional contribution per employee is important to the director. Each employee is generating additional income. The employee business contribution of £11,962 is an average estimate. The director has established a maximum potential and breakeven point based on each employee achieving 37.5 chargeable hours per week and 24.5hrs:

	chargeable hours (per week)	Net profit	employee contribution	contribution per employee
break-even	24.5	£53,460	£0	£0
mid estimate	30	£148,500	£95,700	£11,963
max estimate	37.5	£280,500	£227,700	£28,463

Automation can have the same effect. Manufacturing business will invest heavily in machinery that can carry out tasks more efficiently than a traditional workforce. The same is true in most industries including printing and data processing. Software is now capable of processing thousands of records much quicker and more accurately.

Innovation and being the first to market with a new product or service can revolutionise business sectors.

Example; Think of the way houses are bought today. Almost all of us view houses on-line. The first two national web-based businesses www.rightmove.co.uk and www.zoopla.co.uk capitalised on consumers change in behavior and are still market leaders today and multi-million-pound businesses.

Tax efficiency

Tax evasion is illegal, but tax efficiency will minimise tax payments. Being tax efficient means keeping hold of as much earned money as possible. Being tax efficient is not dishonest. The government expects and encourages people to pay the right amount of tax, it is purely a transactional arrangement. Tax is a necessary expense.

Example; Think about purchasing a dining table. There are many different reasons why customers may buy it, including:

1. It looks good, has good design.
2. It is functional and will fit exactly into a designated space within a customer's home.
3. It is well made, solid and last a long time.
4. It is affordable, cheap, come with free delivery and be within a customer's budget.

Whatever the unique selling point (USP) most customers will be happy if they have purchased the table based on what they want or need.

Imagine you bought a table for £500. As you walk out of the store, the exact same table is offered by a competitor across the street for £250. You might feel that £250 had been wasted.

This is the same when paying tax. It is important to pay the right amount of tax. You don't need to pay £500 if your tax liability is £250.

Understanding your lowest possible personal income before setting up a business is helpful. There are legal elaborate ways to avoid paying tax, but tax is an important part of any country's economy and infrastructure. Government income is essential to fund services, such as the National Health Service and Education. There are however 5 golden rules everyone should know:

1. **Income tax free threshold** – Anyone who is entitled to work in the UK will have a tax-free allowance. In 2019/20 this is £12,500 for every individual. It is particularly important to ensure members of the family utilise this allowance, particularly spouses. The government website: https://www.gov.uk/income-tax-rates will provide information each year.

2. **Business expenses** – Anyone running a business is entitled to deduct expenses wholly and exclusively for the purpose of the business. The government website https://www.gov.uk/expenses-if-youre-self-employed will keep an up to date list of allowable business expenses. Checking is essential prior to a tax return. The four common expenses missed include:
    i. Travel, currently 45p per mile (2019/20).
    ii. Parking.
    iii. Postage and stationary.
    iv. Use of home as a business office.

3. **Efficient purchasing** – It is better not to incur business expenses. If a purchase is necessary specialist comparison websites and apps will help and give confidence that you are paying the lowest possible price. https://www.moneysavingexpert.com/ is one of many websites and consumer forums helping customers get the best deals on a variety of products and services. These are good for business and personal expenses.

4. **Benefits** - Working and child tax credits are available to anyone on a limited income. Everyone who plans to start a business should register, even if you think your income will exceed the threshold. The government website is available for anyone to check eligibility: https://www.gov.uk/tax-credits-calculator.
    a. The https://www.citizensadvice.org.uk/ is also a good resource for other benefits.

5. **Review tax free income** – Some income is not taxable. It is worth considering if you are on a low income or close to the personal income tax free threshold.

Competitions - In the UK unlike the USA, competition prizes are exempt from income tax. Unless an individual actively looks to win prices, sells winnings on a regular basis and earns over the personal tax allowance, income is tax free. Prizes from competition winnings and kept do not form any part of taxable income. Most competitions are free to enter on-line. The most successful "compers" form networks or subscribe to specialist organisations such as:

https://www.compersnews.com/

If you find something - The UK law says you have more right to it than everyone else - except the owner. If the true owner doesn't turn up, you can take ownership. If you are prepared to persevere, there are many examples of "finding things" that have a value where it is unlikely the true owner will appear.

Example; Metal detectors are a way of finding items of value, including money and Jewelry. Ask permission from the landowners first or stick to public places such as parks or the beach.

An allotment is an obvious form of obtaining tax-free goods. People do not pay tax on their home-grown fruit and vegetables and no-one would expect them to. All the food is for their own use. All councils have a legal requirement to made allotments available to the public. A standard plot is 2,722.5 square feet. A standard allotment can cost up to £100 to run per year including seeds. Crops can be grown to the value of £1,000-£2,000 depending on ability and the range of fruit and vegetables grown. You can also swap produce with other allotment owners.

Similar principles apply to sea fishing and foraging e.g. for blackberries, although there are restrictions about taking home some fish and where foraging can take place.

Blogging for personal use to obtain free goods is tax free unless you plan to sell items for profit. Blogging can be a successful way to receive, use and review items. Sometimes bloggers or vloggers can develop to be successful businesses. If you start a blog make a note of any income, because some income may be taxable:

1. Any cash income made from sponsored posts is taxable.
2. Any cash income made from advertising is taxable.

Selling clutter can be a great way to raise additional cash. If you have not used something in the last 6 months the chances are you will not use it in the next 6 months. Some people sell unwanted items on-line, others through car boot sales.

Earning income from **renting out space** such as your home, or a driveway as a parking space is normally taxed. This can be avoided if you effectively swap with someone. There are several home exchange web-based sites where you simply swap your home with another family. The same is true for people who want to avoid parking charges for work. Swapping with someone who works where you live and vice versa is a great way to save money.

Low income earned from hobbies – It is generally accepted that up to £1,000 per year can be earned tax free. The law is not entirely clear, but it is generally accepted that small amounts of income can be made tax free, providing the motive is not profit seeking.

Example; Mrs Smith has an interest in pin-ball machines and antique arcade games. Mr and Mrs Smith attend a fair on the first Sunday of each month. The principle purpose is to build up an interesting collection and speak with other like-minded people.

At the end of the year Mrs Smith believes she has increased the value of her collection from trading pin-ball machines by £1,500. Her extensive knowledge and experience collecting for 20 years has enabled good-value swaps. It has cost Mrs Smith £500 including travel, fair entrance fees and tea and cake. Mrs Smith does not need to declare this income to HMRC.

Writing a business plan

Developing a business plan is important for all new businesses. Either to obtain investment or to act as a company blue-print, a guide. A business plan is a formal written document and gives a company the ability to provide a structure. The business plan will contain goals, how they can be delivered, by who and when.

Business plans should be a fluid document refreshed periodically to remain relevant. The document will inform the directors, investors and staff how the business will function. Everyone involved in the company will be working together and in the same direction of travel. A business plan is a single document underpinned by three principles:

1. **Good business idea** - Must be well explained from the outset in the executive summary. The subsequent chapters will support the idea, be more detailed and explain how the idea will be delivered. The plan will also describe what support will be needed, who is involved and how marketing will generate customers.
2. **Quality Leadership** - The owners and directors of the business must demonstrate their competencies and capabilities to make a success of the business.
3. **Robust financials** - The sales and costs must add-up and be realistic. The pricing structure must represent the value of the service or product being sold and all costs must be included. Most financial plans will include a small start-up contingency budget to cover unexpected items or to budget for start-up costs that overspend.

Good business plans will forge cohesion between the financial targets and corporate behaviours. There will be a clear link between activities carried out by executives and staff and the planned financial delivery.

Example; Imagine you manufacture chocolates and have been told by a friend that cranberries and chocolate make a good combination at Christmas. Your friend suggests you should introduce a new chocolate next year. You speak to other friends who also give positive feedback. Rather than invest thousands of pounds manufacturing a product batch, specific initial activities should be undertaken to prove the idea.

Each activity will have a cost and measured by 3 corporate key performance indicators (KPI's):

1. **Quality and values** - each activity aligned to the company's quality and values policy.
2. **Taste** – Each chocolate must pass the company taste testing guidelines.
3. **Financials** – delivered within cost budget and sales target.

Each initial task will have a financial contribution. After some thought, you decide the best way forward is to make a pilot batch and create a project plan consisting of the elements detailed in the table below.

Activity	Main Cost Contributor	Cost	Income	Quality and Values	Taste	£ Budget
Create a project plan	Time	-£20		✓		✓
Source ingredients (samples)	Materials	-£40		✓		✓
Manufacture samples	Time	-£80		✓		✓
Company tasting event	Time	-£30		✓	✓	✓
Product quality testing	Time	-£60		✓		✓
Financial analysis	Time	-£50		✓		✓
Marketing strategy	Time	-£60		✓		✓
Packaging development	Time	-£60		✓		✓
Consumer tasting/packaging event	Time/ Outsourced	-£60		✓	✓	✓
Product sign-off (directors)	Time	-£60		✓		✓
Source ingredients (main production)	Materials	-£3,000		✓		✓
Manufacture main batch	Time	-£1,000		✓		✓
Cost to sell through in 12wks	Overheads	-£4,000		✓		✓
Expected sales	General Overhead		£20,000	✓	✓	✓
		-£8,520	£20,000			

The structure of the business plan is important and should be well laid out, easy to follow, factual and interesting. Tittle pages may benefit from a picture or company logo and a corporate "footer" will act as a thread. The length of the plan will vary depending on the complexity of the business. As a rule of thumb, short and to the point is better than long and vague. I have found a good length is between 4,000 and 6,000 words with the use of appendices if needed for technical detail and complex sections.

Businesses come in all shapes and sizes. There is no "one size fits all" when it comes to writing a business plan. I have found most business plans can fit into 7 chapters with varying paragraphs:

1. Executive Summary
2. Products and Services
3. Marketing and Lead Generation
4. Competitor Analysis.
5. Company Structure
6. SWOT Analysis
7. Financial Analysis

The next steps are to select the paragraphs and write the content.

Executive Summary (800 – 1,000 words)

Suggested chapters

- Business Idea
- Business Objective

The Executive Summary should be a piece of writing that can stand alone in its own right and is often split into the business idea and objective. The content should include what the business is, where it will be located, who will be involved and how the business will trade. Usually as a sole trader, or limited company.

Describe the business idea and capture the spirit of the plan for the reader including details of where the business idea came from. There may be a problem that the business has found a solution too. The business may provide a service to be delivered in a different or more convenient way for customers.

The company's key milestones can be summarised with details of when they will be completed. This will show a timeline of events. A more detailed project plan may be needed for complex start-ups. Sometimes a simple task list will be enough. It is important to plan and document start-up activities. This will avoid the risk of tasks being missed or duplicated resulting in extra cost.

Businesses looking to secure investment or obtain a business loan, will need to describe the business owners and directors. Detail the contribution each will make to the company, what motivates them and why they are passionate about the business. Investors are looking to ensure they achieve a good return on their investment. They will be looking for good leadership as well as a good idea.

The executive summary should be completed last after all the other chapters. Usually I write a business plan backwards. I start with the financials and highlight all the important points that need to be included in the executive summary.

Products and Services (800 – 1,000 words)

Suggested chapters

- Details of Products and Services
- Pricing Model
- Innovation (if applicable)
- Supplier Analysis (if applicable)
- Corporate Policies (if applicable)
- Dispute Resolution (if applicable)
- Expansion Strategy (if applicable)

The main objective of this chapter is to describe what your product or service is, your delivery model and pricing.

Example; A small retailer may launch with a limited amount of capital and be looking for a low-cost start-up option. Launching on-line before expanding to other channels will enable the company to trade with less start-up capital and lower running costs. The business can trial new ideas and iron out issues before lunching in other channels such as a physical store, pop-up stores or shop-in-shop. Shopping online is convenience for many customers and most online businesses will have lower overheads compared with a traditional "bricks and mortar" model. Starting on-line will be more straightforward than launching with multi-channels.

Typically, profit is generated when a business buys something, adds value to it before selling it on to someone else. The profit element comes from the added value. Adding value to an item or service can be achieved in different ways:

1. Chloe's chocolates source's and purchases ingredients. The manufacturing process transforms the ingredients in to a chocolate adding value and making a desirable product that someone wants to buy.

2. Michelle Hart Life Coaching provides life coaching services. Michelle's experience and training are converted into advice that someone is interested in and prepared to pay for. Experience and training are the added values enables Michelle to provide the service. Michelle could not run her business without her previous work experience and qualifications.

Most service businesses charge customers a fee, often by the hour. To calculate the fee all cost elements will be included, plus the companies desired profit.

Example; A Life coach may charge £75 an hour; this will usually be calculated to include:

1. The direct wages paid to staff members (or director/owner).
2. Cost associated to staff wages such as pension and employer national insurance contributions.
3. Administration and overhead costs, e.g. electricity, rent or equipment.
4. Non-chargeable hours, such as time for invoicing and marketing activities.
5. Travel time and costs including fuel and insurance.
6. Physical purchases made to deliver the service. Including stationary, report binders presented to the client.

Most of this can be calculated in advance to enable easy and quick preparation of written quotes. Hourly assumptions can be made for most costs including wages and overheads. Bespoke costs will need to be calculated with each job.

Suppliers may be important to your business. Some businesses try to keep as much control of their supply chain as possible.

Other businesses try to be "lean" deliberately using third party suppliers. They will lose some control of the supply chain but reduce their fixed costs, such as workforce or premises.

Describing your supply chain model will demonstrate to investors how you intend to buy and sell. Try to avoid models that tie up large sums of cash for long periods. Investors will want to understand how you intend to invest their capital to create revenue. There are much better ways to do this, such as investing in marketing or a salesperson.

If you can, detail your suppliers and why you choose them. If you have not decided yet, describe how you will select a supplier and how your decision will be made. This might include product quality, confidence of supply or unit cost. Most likely all three areas will be considered as part of the decision-making process:

Businesses can fail because of a poor supply chain. A poor supply chain will result in products being out of stock, in the wrong place and having too much of the wrong stock that can't be sold quickly.

High quality, low cost and a good supply chain with short lead-times and products delivered as agreed are all important indicators. How stock is managed is directly connected to financial performance. Sometimes there is a trade-off between these indicators, and it is worth prioritising these according to the importance to your business.

If your product requires high quality, then paying a low price may result in low margins for your supplier. From my experience suppliers will prioritise their customers according to the importance to them, in the same way most businesses do. Paying a low price to your supplier may cost you more in the long run from a poor supply chain. Paying too much for your product leaves you out of pocket with low margins and low profit.

It is better to work with suppliers for the longer term in a partnership. Treating them as important system partners. If necessary, consider agreeing a bonus payment for good quality and on time deliveries.

Consider how stock is purchased. Do you want to have large amounts of cash tied up in stock or would it be better for suppliers to direct ship to your customers? How much confidence do you have in your supplier? Will they deliver to your instructions and will you maintain good relations with your final customer?

Keep a supply risk log and maintain a business continuity plan. This will ensure that if the supply chain fails alternative arrangement can be put in place to mitigate against any financial and reputational risk.

Keep an accurate record of all products in a product catalogue or excel document. If you can, add the standard purchase and current selling price. This will help to ensure stock is priced correctly.

If you are selling hundreds or thousands of products avoid adding each product to the sales forecast. This will become unmanageable. Instead provide a summary of grouped products such as categories. Category names can also be detailed in the product catalogue.

The best way to retain customers is to provide a reason for them to return. This could be through providing high quality customer service, a good range of products or simply through providing good value.

One way to deliver good customer service is through a motivated and well-trained workforce. The business interface with customers is the most important touch-point in all industries. Most businesses understand the importance of this and provide training and a suite of policies to ensure consistency. When things go wrong, having a dispute resolution process will ensure staff are prepared.

Marketing and Lead Generation (1,000 – 1,600 words)

Suggested chapters

- Target Market
- Marketing strategy

When writing a business plan, I dedicate at least a quarter of my time to marketing and research. Many businesses fail in the first year because they are not able to generate enough customers. Many business owners that I speak to underestimate the amount of time it takes to "build a brand". Having a quality product is not always enough. Effective communication, persuading others to buy your product or service is the key ingredient to marketing and gaining customer loyalty.

Who are your products or services for and who is most likely to buy them? Understanding your target market is usually a good starting place. Are you selling direct to consumers or businesses? Are your products targeted to specific demographics? And how are you going to reach them?

Most market research can be conducted on line. Check the quality of the source and the motivation behind it. How does your research fit together, and do you believe it?

I have found most government sources to be reliable. Other sources include nationally recognised industry bodies with a financial and reputation interest in being accurate. I have also used the charity sector such as Age UK or the Citizens Advice. Serious journalism can be useful. Often newspapers or magazines will publish an article and obtain quotes and opinions from industry experts. Using expert opinions to help develop a marketing strategy is accepted providing it is understood that these are expert opinions and not fact. Backing up opinions with data will provide more credibility. The https://www.ons.gov.uk/ or https://www.statista.com/ are probably my most visited websites for checking facts.

Once you have established who your target market is. The next question is how to reach them by developing a marketing strategy. Marketing strategies will be individual for each business, there is no "one size fits all." Once you have created a marketing strategy, give it time to work and build in checkpoints. Develop marketing KPIs and continue to monitor them. It may take time for opportunities to work. Adding checkpoints will enable a business to "pause" and change course if something is not working.

A marketing strategy may include physical materials, such as a brochure, leaflet or poster. Some businesses operate exclusively on-line while others will need to consider both. Most businesses will benefit from a website. The cost of websites has reduced significantly over the last 5 years and can be bought for as little as a few hundred pounds. Businesses may use social media. Companies will often use different platforms tailored to their target market or customer demographics.

Business websites will vary too. Some will contain information only while others enable customers to book or buy a product or service. Most consumers expect a business to be online and have a website/social media presence. How and where will depend on the business and business model.

Many customers move between channels. Some customers look for products and services on-line before visiting a store or showroom. Others visit company premises in person before shopping on-line.

It is important to consider your customers behaviour and shopping preferences before finalising your marketing strategy. It can be effective to develop specific programmes of works, based on the research carried out. Programmes will overlap and share delivery tools. The programmes will work together, be synchronised such as sharing the same strapline or product offers.

Competitor Analysis (300 – 400 words)

Suggested chapters

- Competitors

It is important to understand your competitors, what and how they are selling and where they are based. It can, however, be counterproductive to study them too much or obsess with what they are doing at the expense of developing your own products and innovation. There may be a tendency to copy or imitate a competitor rather than lead the way with new products or services of your own. Make a list of competitors and be mindful of their products, marketing and price points. This is usually enough.

Sometimes a competitor may "do something" or "create something" that can't be ignored.

Example; Even in a local economy a competitor may deliver an advert in a very different or unexpected way. They may use local radio tempting customers away from your business. They might discount to gain market share (loss leaders) or create a new product that is very different and better than anything else on the market.

It is good to review your competitors periodically and assess how their product or service offer has changed and react as necessary.

Company Structure (600 – 1,000 words)

Suggested Chapters

- Team Structure
- Directors
- Premises
- Company Goals and Objectives

This chapter should provide details of how your business will operate effectively. There will be several key tasks that the business needs to carry out to function. This will include activities directly or indirectly linked to income. Tasks may include lead generation, marketing, administration and bookkeeping.

Introduce the directors and provide the most important background information such as previous employment and qualifications. Adding a personal fact or information that motivates can be helpful when trying to obtain investment or a loan. Investors want to know about the individuals they are investing in. They will use their judgment about the company's leadership to help them reach a decision about releasing their investment funds.

Try not to make this section too long and try not to replicate a CV. CV's will be an appendix to any loan or investment application.

If you are trading from premises or you plan to rent office space, provide an much detail as you can including location, budget and size.

Company performance and how to measure it is a very important part of the business plan. Creating key performance indicators (KPIs) will monitor the health of your business. Dividing KPIs into financial and quality will help identify business areas that are performing well and others where improvements need to be made. This may require data to be collected. The effective use of data can be an asset and help with executive decision making.

Think carefully about the data you want to collect and what value it brings to the business. Don't collect information just for the sake of it. Think about how information can be collected and how accurate the data might be. Only by collecting data can you use it to add value.

Example; Unit and sales data by category, selling channel, month and transaction will enable you to measure the financial success of each category and channel, over time. The information can be analysed to understand a variety of useful metrics including:

1. Value of sales in each product category (increasing or decreasing - trend)
2. Units sales in product categories (increasing or decreasing – trend)
3. Sales mix between categories (identifying poor/good performing categories)
4. Average unit sales price (increasing or decreasing - trend)
5. Number of unit sales per transaction (increasing or decreasing - trend)
6. Number of transactions (increasing or decreasing - trend)
7. All the above can be reviewed by selling channel

Financial KPI's are used to determine the financial health of the business. These are mostly lagging indicators reporting on past performance.

Quality KPI's are mostly leading indicators, often more important than financial KPIs. This is because the cost to an established business of poor quality can be catastrophic.

Example; Consider the impact to a business if online customer feedback reduced from a 9/10 rating to 2/10 along with 100 comments of poor quality. Unless action is taken, there is a risk that future financial performance will reduce.

There are important questions to ask about how the business interacts with customers:

1. Does the behaviour of the workforce fit the business culture?
2. Are staff always polite?
3. How do staff attend to detail?
4. How does the behaviour of staff affect sales?
5. How does the behaviour of staff affect customer complaints?
6. Are staff following corporate policies?
7. Do customers know how to make a complaint if something goes wrong?
8. How do staff deal with complaints?

Small businesses tend to overlook quality performance monitoring and for very small business where sales continue to increase, this might be fine. Your business may have a few employees who carry out all the duties. Owners of very small businesses usually know exactly what is going on and intuition is enough.

When the business grows, the owners will naturally lose some control of the culture and quality. Getting this back is best done through setting standards, introducing policies and quality KPI's. This will ensure standards are documented. Through training the workforce will understand them and embed them into their daily activities and culture.

Example; A coffee shop has received double the amount of customer complaints about their time spent queuing. The company handbook already states that customers should not wait more than 4 minutes. The company owner checks the complaints and observes they are all on Sundays. The only day without a senior manager. The policy and KPIs are clear, but the owner recognises that no training has been given to the staff working on Sundays. A 30-minute training session with all staff is scheduled to include corporate policies and demonstrate the importance of providing a timely service to customers. The training will include specific examples showing how this can be achieved by prioritising activities.

SWOT Analysis (100 – 200 words)

Suggested chapters

- SWOT Analysis Table

SWOT refers to strengths, weaknesses, opportunities and threats. No company, even multi-million-pound businesses with market leading products or services can deliver everything they want to. They too have a finite supply of manpower, capacity and money. SWOT analysis will help businesses identify areas of opportunity and risk, dealing in both internal (elements that can largely be controlled) and external (elements that largely can't be controlled) factors.

Example of Strength – The director of a company may already have a list of business contacts that competitors do not have. This is an internal factor and a strength of the business.

Example of Weakness – A new company may not have enough capital to buy equipment or machinery comparable with their competitors. This is an internal factor, resulting in the company being less productive. This may lead to higher costs and less output (lower margin). In this example the company has a choice:

1. To sell product at the same price point as their competitors and accept lower margin
2. To sell product at a higher price point than their competitors, maintain margin at the risk of lower sales.

It might be possible to turn this recognised weakness into a strength by identifying alternative ways of "adding value". If part of the process is handmade, this may add value because hand-made items are perceived to have a high price point. Effective marketing could lead to higher sales mitigating any risk. The business could also consider using alternative ingredients such as natural or organic again "adding value" to the finished product.

Examples of Opportunities – Growing a business may require new opportunities. This could include seeking out a new customer, developing a new product or a different way of delivering a service. An opportunity may include moving to bigger premises or an alternative manufacturing processes may be more productive.

Whatever the opportunity and scale, creating ideas and converting them to credible opportunities is something that all businesses do. In large companies' ideas are often generated through brainstorming. Brainstorming is a group discussion where efforts are made to create ideas or find a solution to a specific problem. In smaller companies' opportunities are often created informally with less structure.

Example; A self-employed window cleaner may be looking for opportunities and decides to deliver leaflets to a new housing estate, creating a new opportunity.

Examples of Threats - A company may choose to buy a product from overseas, paying in $USD. The threat comes from currently fluctuation. This is an external factor and can be mitigated by negotiating a fixed price. The disadvantage of a fixed price is the risk has been transferred to another party who may charge extra for taking on that risk.

Financial Analysis (400 – 800 words)

Suggested chapters

- Start-up summary
- Key assumptions

The financial analysis chapter is a summary of the full financial analysis appendix. I always start with the financials and work backwards through the business plan completing the executive summary last. I revisit the financials at the end of the process to check that the business plan narrative is still compatible with the financial assumptions. Often, I need to adjust the financials either through scaling back / increasing the sales forecast or adjusting some of the overhead costs. The important aspect is to align the financial numbers with the written narrative and recognise the biggest opportunities and risks.

You may need to present the financial numbers to an investor or business partner. Your audience may not understand numbers well, therefore the simpler you can make them the better. If you have complicated calculations, calculate it separately and present the final figure. You can add narrative with details of how the numbers were calculated.

Example; A business may not have secured premises, but a budget needs to be assumed for the business plan. Rents are usually based on size and location of property. A separate table is produced showing various scenarios based on advertised properties. Narrative describes how the final cost budget was assumed.

The financial appendix will have 3 sections, each showing 3 full years:

1. Sales forecast

a. Sales activity forecast
   b. Sales value forecast
   c. Clear phasing
2. Cash-flow
   a. Sales value totals copied from the sales value forecast (Income)
   b. Cost of sales
   c. Overheads
3. Profit and loss

Sales activity forecast – I always start by establishing the maximum sales opportunity of a business.

Example; A "bricks and mortar" retailer can estimate sales based on store location, size, type of retailer and marketing impact.

The owner may wish to visit potential store sites at different times of the day before committing to premises. The purpose is to assess the number of expected customers (footfall)

The calculation could look like this:

1. 1,000 people walk past the store every day
2. 1 out of 10 will enter in the shop: 100 people / day
3. 1 out of 4 people coming to the shop will buy: 25 sales / day
4. the average price of a customer transaction is £13.32: £333 of sales / day
5. the shop is open 30 days a month: £10,000 of sales / month
6. Expected annual turnover £120,000

These figures may vary depending on the day of the week. A Saturday may be busier than a Monday. Calculating the maximum sales potential of a store is done before a bottom up approach can calculate the individual sales by products. The process can be repeated for other sales channels and be added to the store sales total.

Once the maximum sales value has been established, the business can start applying sales to individual products and categories. Where a business has hundreds of products, the products are usually listed in a product catalogue. Only aggregated sales, such as categories are entered in the sales forecast. This will be easier for the sales forecast to be understood and more concise.

Sales by category can be calculated depending on the number of products, price point and expected demand. If the retailer decides to launch with 300 products, recording details of each product and grouping by expected demand in an A, B, C category list can be very useful. This is effectively ranking products by sales or importance

1. A represents the top 20% of products, typically this may represent 60% of total sales.
2. B represents the next 40% of products, typically this may represent the next 30% of sales.
3. C represents the next 40% of products, typically this may represent the final 10% of sales.

Example; An ironmonger's product catalogue might look like this:

Product	Purchase cost (delivered) £	Sales price £	Gross Margin %	Category	A, B, C category
Garden Spade	£11.44	£22.00	92%	Hand tools	A
Garden Folk	£11.44	£22.00	92%	Hand tools	A
Garden Twine	£0.74	£1.50	103%	Accessories	C
Hand trowel	£3.67	£6.00	63%	Hand tools	B
Hand folk	£3.67	£6.00	63%	Hand tools	B
Garden Mower (electric)	£67.00	£99.00	48%	Electric tools	B
Garden Strimmer (electric)	£26.50	£39.00	47%	Electric tools	B

It is important to recognise the sales activity forecast as a forecast, a best estimate based on experience, knowledge or evidence. There may be analytical intelligence based on historical performance or market research. The forecast will be continuously developed and improved over time as information and intelligence is gathered.

Sales value forecast – The sales value forecast takes the expected number of units sold, multiplied by the expected selling price.

Phasing - The business is unlikely to reach the maximum total sales in year 1. It is normal to assume that maximum sales will be reached in year 3 with years 1 and 2 reduced while the business irons out any issues. The sales forecast for years 1 and 2 are set based on a business's starting point. The size of the company's marketing budget, ambition and performance against the quality KPI's are important factures to determine how quickly the company can grow.

Cash-flow – The cash-flow should show the income, less cost of sales and overheads. The summary, usually at the bottom of the page will show the P&L and the rolling cash-flow expected at the end of each month. The month end cash-flow should be positive unless you have a planned overdraft.

The cost of sales are the direct costs associated with the product or service.

Example; A recruitment agency specialising in education may charge schools £30 per hour for a temporary teacher. The teacher is paid £20 per hour. The direct costs would be £20hr + employers national insurance and pension contributions. It may be necessary to apply a contingency percentage to allow for any disputes leading to refunds and extra costs such as travel.

For product-based businesses, allow a contingency for theft, discounts and stock write offs.

Overheads also known as running costs or operating costs will include a wide range of expenses including but not limited to; office rent, equipment, travel and utilities. Directors salaries are also included in the overheads. Other overheads may include support staff such as administration personnel.

Profit and Loss - The profit and loss of the business is then summarised as yearly totals. To check the numbers are showing correctly, the sum of the 3 years profit and capital invested equals the cash total at the end of year 3 in the cash-flow.

Sometimes there are adjustments that need to take place, particularly if stock is purchased.

Example; A retailer purchases £5,000 of stock to fill a store. The £5,000 is reduced in the cash-flow but remains an asset in the business. This is reflected in the profit and loss. Stock adjustments in years 2 and 3 are also reflected in the Profit and Loss.

Chloe's Chocolates Ltd (Business Plan)

Chloe's Chocolates Ltd is a fully written product-based business plan. The plan can be used as an example. The company and owner do not exist in real life.

Executive Summary

Business Idea

Chloe's Chocolates Ltd is a new multi-channel retailer based in Eastbourne. We specialise in artisan chocolates made and packaged with a personal touch. Our business will focus on great **products**, a central **location** and exceptional **customer service**. These three elements will deliver the right product offer to our customers in a growing and lucrative market.

Quality chocolates are key to the success of our business. We will produce a constant supply of high-quality new **products** that our customers will enjoy, coupled with our bestselling core ranges. All chocolates will be developed to our quality guidelines and values during three months of development. Development will include taste testing, ingredient quality, consistency and appearance. Only then will our chocolates meet the perfection required by our founder Chloe Jones.

We will launch with an on-line store www.chloeschocolates.co.uk, an integral part of our business. Our sales pages will be positioned on our homepage. Our physical store **location** has been chosen because of high weekend foot traffic to drive sales. Our ambition is for our store to become distinctive, a destination store where customers will be willing to travel to.

Customer service and excellent product knowledge from all our staff will ensure customers leave with the highest level of satisfaction. Word of mouth is still a very successful form of marketing, a good experience will lead to customers telling their friends. We will develop a repeat-business loyalty scheme to retain customers.

Chloe's Chocolates will trade as a Ltd company owned and operated by Chloe Jones. Chloe is an experienced professional, passionate about quality, chocolate with a personable and energising character. Chloe is the face of our business, creator of great chocolate and an integral part of our brand. Capital requirement is £10,000, financed through personal savings.

Chloe is a serial entrepreneur and recently sold her beauty salon business to a competitor for £300,000. The business was founded in 2007 and expanded to 3 stores in the following 11 years.

Chloe has been making and perfecting chocolates in her spare time for the past three years and developed a range of 30 individual chocolates to be used to launch the business. At the Crockstead Christmas Market in 2018, Chloe sold £700 worth or chocolates to 120 customers in one day of trading. Most sales were boxed chocolates that customers had chosen from the individual assortment. This was the inspiration and evidence Chloe needed to convert her idea into reality.

In three years, our store and website will turnover £133k annually. The artisan chocolate market is lucrative with higher margins than mass-market equivalents. Most chocolate in the UK is consumed by brands that mass produce their chocolate, Cadburys, Mars, Thorntons and Nestle. Sector growth is with smaller upcoming brands such as Hotel Chocolat and Montezuma's.

To manage the business effectively Chloe has developed product categories. The seven categories will enable inventory to be managed better. The category structure will make it easier to identify sales trends in specific groups of products. Most sales will come from our chocolates either as individual units or boxed. To support our core sales other categories will be introduced such as cards and gifts to provide add-on sales.

Chloe's Chocolates will be divided in to seven categories:

- Chocolates (Individual)
- Chocolates (Boxed)
- Chocolates (Seasonal)
- Cards
- Wrapping paper, gift boxes and accessories
- Gifts
- Other

Chloe is an ambitious entrepreneur with creative ideas to expand the business through innovation and opportunity. Once the core chocolate business has established, Chloe will introduce a chocolate party making programme. Chloe has identified an opportunity to offer parties to children between the ages of 6 and 15. Other ideas include a loyalty scheme and form partnerships with local high street stores to generate shop-in-shop sales. In year 3 Chloe will conduct a full business review and produce an expansion business case.

Business Objective

The principle business objective is to launch a premium artisan chocolate brand in East Sussex. Chloe has identified an empty store in Eastbourne approx. 200 square feet. We will create a friendly and authentic store, with signage providing product information to customers. We will promote storytelling and display interesting facts about our ingredients giving customers a connection to our chocolates.

Our three objectives:

1 - Provide customer service second to none. We have a customer first policy.

2 - Core and seasonal products of the highest quality, delicious and attractive.

3 - Offer multi-channels and a convenient retail experience; in-store, online, trade-events, seasonal fairs, chocolate making parties/events and in time shop-in-shop.

We have developed a 3-year strategy summarised below:

Year	Key Business Developments
1	**Phase I (First 6 Months)** - Launch our store with a press event, inviting friends and representatives from the community - Develop a new website (including information pages) - Launch our chocolate making party programme - Increase online social presence on Facebook and Twitter - Launch competitions and customer surveys - Implement a loyalty scheme - Develop a trade-event diary - Develop a seasonal range plan - Apply to win an award dedicated to chocolate - review company goals and objectives **Phase II (Next 6 Months)** - Achieve £57k sales in year 1 - Attend trade-events - Further refine chocolate making party programme - Continue to review company goals and objectives
2	- Achieve £82k in sales in year 2 - Consider registration for VAT - Continue to review company goals and objectives
3	- Achieve £133k in sales in year 3 - Develop an expansion strategy, including shop-in shop opportunities - Continue to review company goals and objectives

Products and Services

Details of Products

Our company will retail chocolates and supporting accessories such as gifts, balloons, cards, gift boxes and wrapping paper. We will also trade locally at fairs and specialist food markets. Chloe will create a diary of trade-events where chocolates will be sold direct to the public. The events will be selected based on their alignment to our brand.

We have structured our business into seven sales categories:

Individual chocolates. Individually our chocolates will sell by weight, approx. two chocolates for £1. Based on pilot sale trials, we have estimated the average number of individual chocolates per transaction will be five. Our core range will consist of 30 chocolates, strictly controlled by Chloe. Maintaining a range of 30 core chocolates will ensure a high rate of sale. Expired/damages are kept to a minimum. Inventory will be managed effectively.

Individual boxed. We will keep two core boxed chocolates each containing 12 chocolates retailing for £6. One will contain nuts, the other will be nut free. We will not be able to guarantee a nut free chocolate, because of the way our chocolates are manufactured. We will also keep a third option for customers to pick-their-own from the individual range.

Seasonal Chocolates. Chloe will set aside time to develop a seasonal range aligned to the seasonal range development plan. This will require a project approach and include:

- Chocolate development
- Chocolate testing (to quality guidelines)
- Chocolate manufacture

- Sales period, including any mark downs and/or promotions

Cards. Chloe has identified a greetings card supplier and is in advanced discussions. Our plan is for the supplier to stock their product range within our store. Chloe's Chocolates will collect a % of sales from each transaction. This will provide additional income without being tied to stock control and other functions that may distract from our core business.

Wrapping paper and gift boxes. Chloe has agreed to purchase inventory from a local supplier and will apply a 50% mark-up. By purchasing stock Chloe will have complete control over the colours and designs of the gift boxes and wrap. This will ensure our range is coloured and designed to enhance our core chocolates. This category also includes balloons and gift tags from the same supplier.

Gifts. Our gift category is less worked up than others. We will hold a range of gift products that have a relationship to chocolate. Gifts may be chocolate themed or connected with the experience of enjoying chocolates. Items will include mugs, hot water bottles and candles. Chloe has been unable to find a gift supplier and as a result an entry has been made on the company risk register.

There is a risk that gifts will not be available at store launch unless a suitable gift supplier can be found. Chloe has asked her good friend to help her. Sarah Flowers works in retail and has a good understanding of what Chloe is trying to achieve with her business. Sarah has agreed to source suitable suppliers and shortlist three for Chloe to review.

Other. Chloe is working on an exciting and innovative programme of work to create chocolate making parties. The parties will be suitable for everyone adults and kids, but principally children between the ages of 6-15. Chloe is also considering a drop-in style arrangement at our store and the ability to be mobile.

Full details are contained within our chocolate making party structure document. Our parties will provide additional sales and a marketing opportunity to build awareness of our chocolates and brand.

In order to build loyalty and keep customers informed, customers will be sent regular update emails. A loyalty system will be implemented with a points system to reward higher spending. Loyal customers will receive discounts as well as be given the opportunity to preview new product ranges.

The use of samples during busy times will introduce customers to new flavours.

Pricing Model

Our standard pricing policy will be kept simple to ensure all items are priced correctly and there are no mistakes. The pricing model has been derived using the following criteria:

- A bottom up approach to calculate an appropriate retail price per item.
- A benchmark approach comparing similar products from competitors.

The table below sets out the average retail price per unit over the first 3 years of trading. We will apply a 5% price increase in years two and three:

Categories	Average Retail Price Year 1	Average Retail Price Year 2	Average Retail Price Year 3
Chocolates (5 individual)	£2.50	£2.63	£2.76
Chocolates (Boxed)	£6.00	£6.30	£6.62
Chocolates (Seasonal boxed)	£10.00	£10.50	£11.03
Cards	£1.80	£1.89	£1.98
Wrapping paper, gift boxes and accessories	£1.50	£1.58	£1.65
Gifts	£7.00	£7.35	£7.72
Other	£3.00	£3.15	£3.31

Lower prices in year one will provide an opportunity to develop loyal customers before increasing prices to their true market value by year 3.

We have prepared analysis regarding the number of customer transactions, average transaction value and how this relates to a typical day. The table below shows our plans over the first three years:

	Year 1	Year 2	Year 3
Customer transactions	12,694	17,532	26,916
Average transaction value	£4.50	£4.73	£4.96
Trading days	312	312	312
Transactions per day	41	56	86
Income per day	£183	£266	£428
Annual income	£57,121	£82,837	£133,535

Marketing and Lead Generation

Market Research

According to www.luxuo.com the **Top 5 chocolate consuming countries** in 2012, based on per capita consumption were:

1. Switzerland 11.9 kg
2. Ireland 9.9 kg
3. UK 9.5 kg
4. Austria 8.8 kg
5. Belgium 8.3 kg

The value of online sales of chocolate is difficult to quantify. All the specialist manufacturers/retailers of chocolate, such as Hotel Chocolat and Montezuma's have a significant on-line presence.

www.ajcn.nutrition.org have produced a paper about the patterns of chocolate consumption. Men consume more chocolate than women up to the age of 30. After 30, Women are the greatest consumers of chocolate, before consumption evens out again after retirement.

Most chocolate is consumed by people between 12 and 40. There is also a seasonal difference in the consumption of chocolate with nearly twice as much chocolate consumed in winter than summer.

According to www.statista.com the overall retail sales of chocolate in the UK has reduced from its peak in 2008 but has been steady at around £4B for the last seven years. Evidence has shown that the UK economy declined shortly after 2008. Other factors are said to be a growing awareness of the benefit of a healthy diet. Chocolate is a well-established, popular luxury food in the UK.

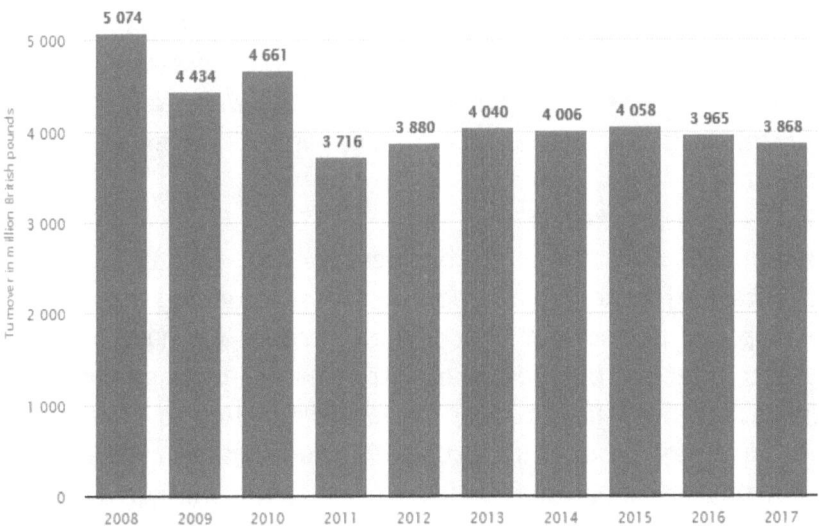

In 2017 the telegraph wrote an article about consumers moving away from mass produced chocolate to higher quality artisan chocolate. With Cadburys reporting a drop-in-sales by 4.2% in 2017, smaller bands are moving in with personally designed bespoke products.

In summary

- The chocolate market in the UK is around £4B.
- The UK is the third largest consumer of chocolate (by population) in the world.
- The market has seen a shift from mass produced brands to smaller artisan chocolates.
- All ages and genders enjoy chocolate.
- The gift market is important within the industry.
- Sales are seasonal with higher sales in the colder month. Christmas and Easter sales are vital.

Marketing Strategy

The effective use of technology will make the business streamlined and efficient. The website will be outsourced but maintained by Chloe's Chocolates Ltd. Chloe will have easy access to all areas to make amendments as and when needed. The website is responsive meaning it is fully accessible on PC, laptop, tablet and mobile platforms.

The principle objective of our business over the first 12 months will be to gain a foothold in Eastbourne and surrounding area. We will develop and perfect our chocolates to ensure we have a credible product offer for our customers. Transparent pricing, exceptional service and a quality product range, all qualities to maintain our core customer base. Our focus will include online marketing and direct physical marketing linked to our target market. Chloe has identified and costed a marketing strategy to be delivered under eight programmes:

The digital marketing business has become a lucrative and global industry with hundreds of specialist companies offering specific services. The industry has particularly grown in the last 5 to 10 years. Freelance options are available through a number of websites including www.peopleperhour.com and www.freelancer.co.uk. These are cheaper, but often with similar technical solutions. The right freelancer will be just as effective and offer good return on investment.

Our Chosen freelance professional will focus on the following areas:

- Search marketing
- Social marketing
- Pay per click management
- Banner advertising
- Improved conversion rates
- E-mail direct marketing

E-Mail direct marketing works best when potential customers are targeted and considered relevant for our market. We will create a database of customers and potential customers and connect appropriately. We will include a newsletter and simple effective email messaging. Our database will be fed with information from:

- All forms of social media
- Questionnaires
- Existing customers
- Connections at events
- Competitions

Social media will be used to market our website. Presence across the social media spectrum will include Facebook and Twitter.

Facebook Marketing. There will be innovative content and an exciting user experience with a responsive and consistent message (posts – likes, share and comments). Users are updated with new and engaging product offers using videos and colour to drive traffic to our website.

Why is Facebook important for us?

There are over 1.44 Billion users of Facebook, and still the biggest social media tool on the internet.

Every popular brand is on Facebook why?

- Customer Interaction
- Give a personal touch to your business
- Develop a loyal fan base
- Beat your competition
- Viral promotion

Twitter Marketing. There will be interesting content, engaging user experience, responsive and consistent message (hash tags, following and tweets /re-tweets). Users are updated with new and engaging tweets about our products and offers to drive traffic to our website. Once a tweet reaches a certain level and size (number of users), the message would be used to reach a wider audience.

Chloe's Chocolates will select a digital marketing expert through a robust selection process. We will ensure the "best fit" for our business, working to strict "terms of engagement." Payment will be on results.

Networking events. The key benefits of these event are to network with peers and spend valuable face-to-face time with potential customers. There are many chocolate festivals throughout the UK. Manchester holds the largest festival in the UK each January chocolate-festival-manchester

Other events can be found at:

- eventbrite.com
- foodfestivalfinder.co.uk

Chloe will review the online schedules periodically and create an event diary. Attendance will either be through purchasing a stand or attendance to gain ideas. Event marketing can be an efficient and cost-effective way to increase brand awareness and gain customers. A short strategy document will be prepared in advance to ensure key people are seen and time is effective.

Customer referrals. Providing a good customer experience is the best and cheapest way to enhance our brand and maintain our customer base. In a highly technical world, word of mouth is still a very credible marketing strategy. Customer referrals work best when our customers feel naturally part of our brand, usually when they have received a good customer experience. Our marketing will be effective when customers are "nudged."

At the end of a sales transaction, customers will have an opportunity to provide feedback consisting of a short 30 second survey. Upon completion, customers will be entered in to a draw to win a £100 gift voucher. The benefits include:

- A great way to collect customer data.
- Customer feedback, essential to improving our customer offer.
- Customers will feel connected to our brand.
- Customers may feel they are getting something for nothing.

Instore physical marketing. We will use a high impact physical promotional campaign that will generate customer interest. Storytelling about our products and ingredients will provide interesting and engaging narrative.

The www.telegraph.co.uk/health-fitness/nutrition/chocolate published an article recently detailing 10 reasons why good quality chocolate is good for you. Chloe's chocolate is good for you and tastes amazing. During busy trading periods samples will be offered to customers browsing through our store.

Local Marketing events. We will establish a calendar and get involved in local events such as community fairs, school fates and food festivals. Chloe's Chocolates will generate a local presence and it's an opportunity to generate local brand awareness.

Loyalty scheme. We will consider options for a loyalty scheme to reward regular customers with discounts and offers.

Blogging and testimonials. Blogging has become an essential form of marketing for many industries. There are now bloggers in all specialist sectors, including the food industry.

What is a blog? A blog article is a testimonial written by an Industry expert providing a favourable view on a product, service or brand. Our aim will be to digitally drive our target market within customer's normal on-line experience through the blog article to our website.

This is a relatively cost-effective form of marketing, something that will be tested and evolve over time. We will aim to work with partners, and select a core group of professionals such as those found on:

- https://www.vuelio.com/uk/social-media-index/top-10-uk-food-blogs/
- https://detailed.com/food-blogs/
- https://blog.feedspot.com/chocolate_blogs/

Awards. Nothing sells a business better than recognition. An award will provide further opportunities and give our future marketing initiatives greater impact. The business will specifically target an appropriate award and dedicate specific time and resources to win. Our focus will be on chocolate:

- http://www.academyofchocolate.org.uk/awards/
- https://www.internationalchocolateawards.com/

Competitor Analysis

Competitors

Our competitors will sell chocolate in the same way that we do. Most will sell in store and on-line. Some will sell complimentary products, such as gifts or be part of a café. Our differential is exclusive chocolates made from the finest ingredients, blended together by our founder Chloe. The table below shows a list of some of Chloe's Chocolates' closest competitors:

Company	Comment
sweetmoments.co.uk	Have you ever been disappointed by the quality of chocolate products generally available? Have you gone to a so-called specialist supplier and found the price to be astronomical? These are exactly the reasons that in 2003 Vic and Karen opened a small Belgian chocolate shop in Seaford, East Sussex called Sweet Moments, where you can buy some of the finest quality chocolates imported from Belgium at excellent prices.

Company	Comment
hotelchocolat.com	In 2003, Choc Express rebranded as Hotel Chocolat and launched its first retail store in the centre of Watford. The company then grew initially to having four stores in the East Anglian area, with stores in Milton Keynes, Cambridge and St Albans opening between 2005 and 2006. Today, the company has over 70 around the UK. In 2006, the company officially acquired the Rabot Estate in Saint Lucia, and is, to date, the only company in the UK to own its own cocoa plantation. This plantation is one of the reasons given for the company choosing not to be Fair Trade-accredited, as only smallholdings are allowed.

Company	Comment
deliciouslygorgeous.co.uk	Whether you are enjoying a family trip to the seaside, having a day out shopping at the Arndale Centre, looking for a special gift or something yummy for yourself, treating a loved one to afternoon tea or just catching up with friends, Deliciously Gorgeous has something for you. All our products are of the finest quality, and our highly trained staff will prepare your order promptly, giving you more time to enjoy a quick bite in your lunch hour or spend an afternoon sipping hot coffee and chatting with your friends. After a short while, Deliciously Gorgeous the cake designer became Deliciously Gorgeous the confiserie (or confectioner) with the addition of our chocolate counter, where we sell fine Belgian chocolates.

Company Structure

Team Structure

The business will run under the directorship of Chloe Jones who will remain accountable and oversee all the business duties. Specialist tasks will be outsourced, and some activities may be carried out in partnership with a specialist company, such as marketing.

The key tasks will include:

- The manufacture of chocolates, bespoke to Chloe's Chocolates Ltd.
- The management of our store in Eastbourne.
- Development or our marketing strategy to grow the business.

The table below sets out the business activities by task:

Activity	Directors	Part-time assistant	Advisor	Outsourced
Bookkeeping	✓			
Accounting				✓
Legal				✓
Administration	✓			
Marketing and lead generation	✓	✓		✓
Marketing events	✓	✓		
Branding	✓			✓
Store sales	✓	✓		
Online sales	✓	✓		
Stock management and ordering	✓			
Chocolate manufacturing	✓			✓
New product design	✓	✓	✓	
Quality control	✓		✓	
Corporate governance	✓		✓	

Our business will require part-time shop assistants to cover for the director from time to time. Our store will be open 6 days a week. Our staff will be paid a premium aligned to the responsibility of opening and running the store on elected days:

Year 1   £500 per month or 55.5hrs at £9 per hour
Year 2   £750 per month or 83.3 hrs at £9 per hour

Year 3   £1,125 per months or 125 hrs at £9 per hour

The table below shows how wages are divided between workforce pay, employers NI and pension contributions:

	Pay (per hour)	Employer NI contribution 7% (per hour)	Employer pension contribution 3% (per hour)	Total cost (per hour)
Sales assistant	£8.18	£0.57	£0.25	£9.00

Director

Chloe Jones founder and director. Chloe is a serial entrepreneur having run her own Hair and Beauty Saloon for 11 years and responsible for five staff. Chloe now wants to develop a business dedicated to her passion, chocolate. Chloe has been making chocolate for three years. Starting as a hobby, she has perfected her skills working alongside her mum in her kitchen.

Chloe is well known locally for beautiful crafted homemade chocolates that she currently sells to friends and at local food markets. Following this success and completing her qualification in Catering and Hospitality NVQ level 3, Chloe feels this is the right time to start Chloe's Chocolates Ltd.

Steve Flowers Adviser. Steve has been a good friend to Chloe for 20 years and runs a successful plumbing and heating engineering business. The business has been in profit for 5 consecutive years and now employs a workforce of 10. While not employed by Chloe's Chocolates, Steve will be on hand to answer any questions and provide advice should the need arise.

Premises

The registered trading address for Chloe's Chocolates is 15 Blackberry lane, Eastbourne, East Sussex. Chocolate manufacture will take place in our extended home kitchen, with dedicated space for chocolate manufacture throughout the day.

We have selected a fully serviced store with enough local community support and foot traffic to drive sales and a small space to the rear to process online orders. The fully serviced property of approx. 200 square feet is available to rent within our budget of £600 per month.

Where possible the director will design the store layout in a way that provides a natural flow for customers. Store fitting will be sourced from one of several discounted suppliers like:

http://www.shopfittingwarehouse.co.uk

Fitting will take place prior to store opening during a two-week period. This is enough time to ensure the store looks perfect before launch.

Company Goals and Objectives

Every month the director will review the company's financial performance through a set of indicators. These key performance indicators (KPI's) will be introduced to monitor against the business plan. Changes will be made as necessary to take advantage of good performance and address any issues.

This will include but not limited to:

Sales

- Total sales v plan
- Category sales v plan
- Sales by price point
- Number of customers
- Number of repeat customers
- Number of new customers and where they heard about our company
- Average transaction value
- Average sales margin v plan
- Performance of marketing events
- Sales by individual chocolate
- Number of core product lines for sale (at any one time)
- Number of seasonal product lines for sale (at any one time)
- Value of stock holding

Quality

- Customer feedback (through questionnaires)
- On-line profile rating

- Number of customer complaints (with reasons)
- Performance of customer taste tests
- Number of item returns

The data will be analysed monthly and will form an important element to the success of the business. There are three principle reasons for this.

- To provide assurance to the director that the company is achieving the sales and profit outlined in the business plan.
- To provide assurance that all categories of the business are achieving their maximum potential.
- To provide assurance that future lead generation initiatives and marketing events are targeted in areas to generate the greatest return on investment (ROI). And return on directors' time.

For the first year we will focus on "building the brand" and "increasing the number customers."

SWOT Analysis

SWOT Analysis Table

Chloe has created a SWOT analysis based on her experience as a director of a successful beauty salon chain. The business will review the SWOT periodically to ensure that opportunities are realised, and risks identified:

Strengths	Weaknesses
Commitment to providing exceptional customer service	Limited advertising budget compared with our competitors
Target customers have high customer loyalty	Unknown brand.
Community events	
Good location for target market.	
Established relationships with ingredient suppliers	
Opportunities	**Threats**
Establishing a database of customers	Competition, big well-known companies and established local competitors
Gift ranges + seasonal	
On-line sales	
Shop-in-shop opportunities	
Awards	

Financial Analysis

Start-up Summary

The business requires an initial investment of £10,000 which the director has put into the company as a company loan. This investment is enough to start the business and gain a foothold within Eastbourne and the surrounding area.

The initial investment will be used to develop the business infrastructure including a website, system development, branding, secure premises and implement our marketing strategy. The business is expected to make a small profit in the first two years with initial revenue to be reinvested. The director can complete most of the on-line start-up activities although some tasks will be outsourced, such as website development:

Item	Start-up
Chocolate Manufacture	£3,500
Store purchases	£1,500
Computer (laptop) +broadband	£700
Shop fit and store front	£1,500
Website and online maintenance	£1,500
Contingency	£1,300
Total	£10,000

Our rented store is approx. 200 square feet. Small enough to provide a personal service to customers. Large enough to stock a full range of chocolates, gifts and related categories.

Key Assumptions

Details of all sales activity, expenditure, cash-flow and profit and loss have been provided in the financial appendix. The table below shows a summary of how the financials are expected to look over the first 3 years of trading.

	Year 1	Year 2	Year 3	Total
Sales	£57,121	£82,837	£133,535	£273,492
Cost of sales	-£24,047	-£32,776	-£51,332	-£108,156
Gross profit	£33,074	£50,060	£82,202	£165,336
Gross Margin	58%	60%	62%	
Overheads	-£28,096	-£37,633	-£48,133	-£113,862
Inventory (increases)	£5,000	£0	£0	£5,000
Net profit	£4,978	£12,427	£34,070	£56,474
Net Margin	8.7%	15.0%	25.5%	

Chloe will keep the businesses financial performance in constant review. The cash-flow of the business will be an important element and reviewed monthly.

The sales forecast has been created using several realistic assumptions. The assumptions range from the number of items sold per category, through to the expected realised value. These include:

- Reduced income in the early years to allow the business time to grow and iron out any difficulties that may arise.
- Unit sales of 17k in year 1 increasing to 37k in year 3.
- Average unit sales value of £3.28 increasing to £3.57 in year 3.
- Customer numbers increase from 12,694 in year 1 to 26,916 in year 3.

- Average transaction value (ATV) increases from £4.50 in year 1 to £4.96 in year 3
- Part-time staff recruited from launch, additional staff will be required to cover time off for the director
- Chocolate manufacture costs reduce from 28% of retail value to 25% in year 3
- Bought in store purchases such as cards, ribbon, gift boxes reduce from 50% to 45% of retail value.
- A 5% contingency cost has been applied to cover write-offs, discounts and theft.
- Gross margin increases from 58% in year 1 to 62% in year 3
- Sales value to achieve £133k in year 3, a good yet realistic income for a store of 200 square feet.
- Online sales increasing from 10% in year 1 to 30% in year 3

The primary objective of the business is to provide quality range of chocolates for any occasion, and an outstanding friendly service.

Michelle Heart Life Coaching Ltd (Business Plan)

Michelle Heart Life Coaching Ltd is a fully written service-based business plan. The plan can be used as an example. The company and owner do not exist in real life.

Executive Summary

Business Idea

Michelle Heart Life Coaching delivers specialist life coaching services to private individuals and staff within major organisations. Our founder, Michelle Heart has been planning and preparing to launch her business using her wealth of skills and experience. She is a business executive specialising in Human Resources with experience overseeing a workforce of 400. Michelle is a qualified transformation coach and an advisor to the local Citizen's Advice branch.

Michelle understands first-hand how to make a difference to people's lives through warm engagement. Her coaching techniques allow clients to open-up and discover parts of themselves they had lost or forgotten. Specialising in lifestyle improvement through relationships and corporate development, Michelle will help clients to understand who they are and release their limitations often holding them back.

In the past Michelle has suffered from loneliness, a complex and usually unpleasant emotional response to isolation. Loneliness typically leads to anxious feelings and a lack of connection to people. Michelle has an interest in the subject and studied loneliness as part of her master's degree.

A recent report from the office of national statistics: ons.gov.uk has suggested that 5% of the population of England often or always feel lonely, with the prevalence higher in women. There are 700,000 adults living with autism. According to autism.org.uk autistic people are 4 times more likely to feel lonely.

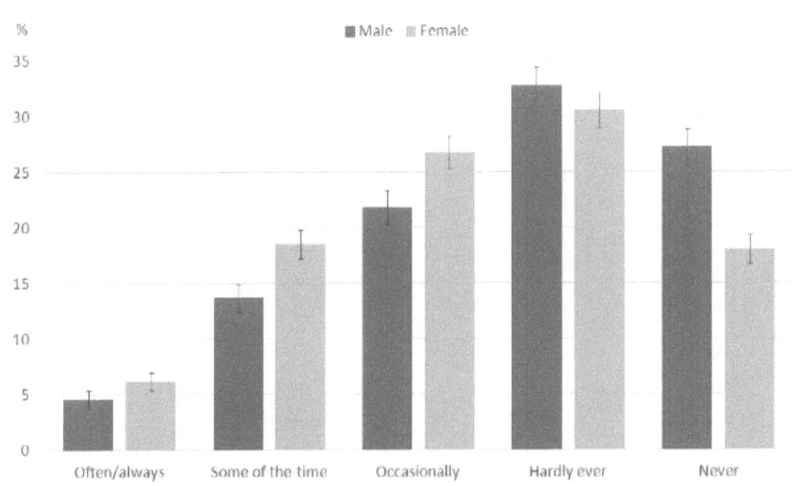

Source: Community Life Survey, August 2016 to March 2017

Michelle believes there is a connection between loneliness and happiness. Reducing the effects of loneliness will increase client's confidence to form meaningful relationships. Happiness is a human state often taken for granted, but not usually fully understood. It is difficult to quantify a level of happiness and studies have shown it difficult to achieve and maintain.

Following a feasibility study, Michelle has identified life coaching as a growing business sector. Michelle will specialise in:

- Lifestyle improvement (relationships and quality of life – happiness.
- Life-restructuring (managing change.)
- Corporate development.

There are many business coaches based in Portsmouth, so Michelle intends to target individual clients with a lifestyle improvement or restructuring need. Michelle's focus will be relationship development. Happiness, loneliness and confidence.

Things that can make you happy:

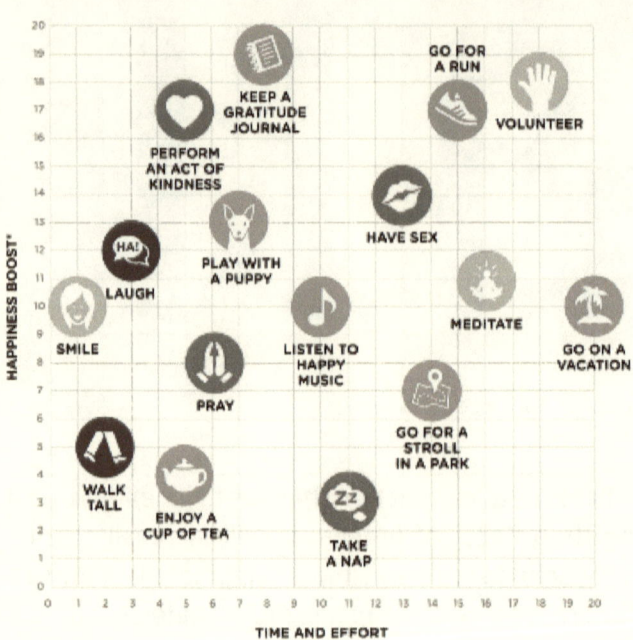

Michelle Heart Life Coaching will trade as a Ltd company. The company will launch in June 2019 as a provider of life coaching and related consultancy services. A personal investment of £10,000 will fund the start-up expenditure including:

Website
System development
Branding
Securing office premises
Implementation of our marketing strategy

Our marketing strategy has been specifically developed to take the business from a modest turnover in year 1 of £39k to £93k in year 3.

We will register for VAT once the threshold of £85,000 turnover has been reached in any 12-month period.

It is expected to take 3 years to develop our business, iron out any issues and be confident to expand. During year 3 Michelle will develop an options appraisal and business case for expansion. The focus will be within the following areas, but fully recognise the need to be responsive to market conditions:

- Creation of self-help products and apps.
- Expand to other areas of the UK, employ life coaches and work closer with business partners. Seek ways to monetise them.
- Expand on the corporate side including speaking opportunities and collaboration with large corporations.

Business Objective

The success of the business will depend on specific factors that have been incorporated into our business model:

Clear, concise marketing to attract clients targeted to our market.
Open and transparent pricing.
Customer service second to none.
Outcomes based approach with client follow-up.

Michelle Heart Life Coaching Ltd will be highly profitable inside 3 years through our sound marketing strategy and effective partnerships. Our 3-year plan with milestones is summarised below:

Year	Key Business Goals
1	**Phase I (First 6 Months)** - Develop a new website (including information pages) - Launch in Portsmouth and surrounding area - Launch new marketing strategy - Engage with affiliates and partnership organisations - Select and work with a digital marketing professional - Review company goals and objectives - Attend at least 1 networking event - Apply to win a coaching award **Phase II (Next 6 Months)** - Achieve £39k in sales in year 1 - Expand throughout Hampshire and Sussex - Develop key affiliates and partnerships - Consider employment of a personal assistant - Win a coaching award - Continue to review company goals and objectives

Year	Key Business Goals
2	- Achieve £78k in sales in year 2
- Launch in 2 further counties across the UK
- Win 2 coaching awards
- Continue to review company goals and objectives
3	- Achieve £93 in sales in year 3
- Win 3 coaching awards
- Write an expansion options paper and business case
- Continue to review company goals and objectives

Products and Services

Details of Product/Services

Michelle Heart Life Coaching offers a comprehensive coaching service to individuals. Inspiration has come from Michelle's observations of the sector. The demand for coaching has increased significantly in recent years, largely due to the complex and often difficult lifestyles people lead.

While some coaches use email and telephone to communicate with clients, Michelle prefers to meet face-to-face. Certainly, for new clients meeting face-to-face is more effective. Michelle will be able to understand her clients body language, meeting face to face helps to develop trust. It is also appreciated by clients; they will appreciate the extra trouble to build a stronger professional relationship.

Reputation will be built upon providing the highest quality coaching to deliver the best outcome. Michelle is proud of the rigorous internal Quality Assurance Systems she has developed that will be continually reviewed and monitored. These systems are supported by her governing body "Association for Coaching".

Services have been packaged into bundles to provide added value and a clear pricing structure. Sessions can be bought individually or as one of three packages moon, earth and sun:

- Individual sessions
- Moon package (3 sessions)
- Earth package (6 sessions)
- Sun package (12 sessions)

The packages will be agreed with the client before service commencement and based on individual need and complexity.

Within 12-months, Michelle will employ a personal assistant. At first on a part-time basis, increasing to full time in year 3. The employment will support Michelle to maximise the number of chargeable hours achieved. The personal assistant will be responsible for vital back office functions including, but not limited to:

- Managing Michelle's diary, including client meetings, travel time, client preparation and report writing
- Dealing with queries
- New client questionnaires
- Proof reading
- Management of website
- Invoice management
- Administration
- Bookkeeping

Effective delivery of our business model requires structure. Michelle has developed a pathway process to ensure clients flow effectively from the initial advertising through to service commencement.

Applying a pathway process will allow us to record progress and ensure clients receive their first session within 14 days. Michelle and her team will follow six process steps:

1. Advertising (through online, print and word of mouth)

2. Clients call (an informal chat. Michelle may need to call the client back)

3. Questionaire (e.mailed to client, returned and reviewed)

4. Preporation of coaching plan (tailored to indevidual needs - use subject plans)

5. Sessions agreed (scheduled with client including terms of enguagement)

6. Review of the plan (service commencement)

All clients will follow a bespoke coaching plan, to meet their specific needs. Michelle has prepared standard subject plans in common coaching areas.

These subject plans will be used and adapted to form a bespoke client plan. The content of each will be based on the initial phone consultation and client questionnaire. Further subject plans will be written as and when needed and electronically stored in a repository:

1. Overcome stress, depression and anxiety
2. Gain confidence, motivation and energy
3. Career improvement or transition
4. Getting that dream job
5. Loneliness
6. Happiness
7. Dealing with relationships
8. Health and fitness
9. Understanding your limitations
10. Positive psychology
11. Dealing with financial matters
12. Time savings

13. Making a dream happen
14. Self believe and greater confidence

For **large organisations and businesses** provision will vary. Michelle Heart Life Coaching is very committed to providing a quality service to all individuals and stakeholders. Michelle will engage with company executives to establish the "need" of each organisation, create a plan and set fees accordingly.

Group sessions can be provided. However, Michelle recognises client's individual needs and acknowledges that everyone is different. Recognising, understanding and tailoring individual needs is a key selling point, a message throughout our branding and strapline.

Feedback will be received from all customers, private individuals and corporate clients. A short questionnaire will enable Michelle to understand what works well and identify areas for improvement.

Pricing Model

Our pricing model has been derived using the following criteria:

- A bottom up approach to calculate an appropriate chargeable hour (£50 to £75.)
- A benchmark approach comparing similar organisations and market conditions.

The table below shows the expected sales fees by package:

Categories	Average Retail Price (hr) Year 1	Average Retail Price Year (hr) 2	Average Retail Price (hr) Year 3	Chargeable hr rate
Individual sessions	£75.00	£75.00	£75.00	£75.00
Moon package (3 sessions)	£195.00	£195.00	£195.00	£65.00
Earth package (6 sessions)	£330.00	£330.00	£330.00	£55.00
Sun package (12 sessions)	£600.00	£600.00	£600.00	£50.00

Michelle Heart life Coaching will charge by the hour, aligned to the number of sessions purchased. Michelle will need to schedule evenings and weekends to meet client's needs.

Michelle will account for every hour worked, chargeable and non-chargeable. Initially Michelle will have fewer clients. Most of her time will be spent on non-chargeable activities such as marketing and lead generation. As the business develops this will reverse. An increase in clients will lead to an increase in chargeable hours. For the business to be successful, Michelle will need to achieve 7 chargeable hours each working day. The table below shows how chargeable hours will increase over the first 3 years:

	Year 1				Year 2				Year 3			
	Q1	Q2	Q3	Q4	Q1	Q2	Q3	Q4	Q1	Q2	Q3	Q4
Chargeable hours	84	150	216	279	301	345	387	417	429	429	429	429
Non-chargeable hours	357	291	225	162	140	96	54	24	12	12	12	12
Total hours	441	441	441	441	441	441	441	441	441	441	441	441

Service Policies

Michelle has developed a set of policies covering all areas of our consultancy services. This is to ensure a consistent and high-quality approach with all clients. Policies will be regularly reviewed and updated every 3 years or when new legislation requires a policy change. All policies are stored on the library section of our company online folders in the following categories:

- Client planning
- Communication
- Health and safety
- Human resources
- Quality assurance
- Governance

Michelle will complete all mandatory training aligned to her membership professional body, Association for Coaching. The training will enable Michelle to be kept up to date with all the necessary policy changes.

Dispute Resolution

It is expected that our packages will offer great value for customers. Our objective is to deliver customer service second to none and we will take all measures to avoid customer complaints including:

- Agreed terms of reference with every client.
- Keep records of all coaching sessions and provide a client report.

We have written a dispute resolution policy (DRP) that will form part of our terms and conditions of business. Customers will know how to make a complaint and who to make it to.

Expansion strategy

By year 3 we will have perfected our services and generated a good level of income. We will have created a database of clients and made a list of potential ideas for expansion.

Our expansion will be formed of two parts. The first to deliver company profit, the second to expand our corporate values through campaigns. Michelle will write an expansion strategy document to support income and campaigns:

Company Profit	Corporate Values
<ul><li>Identify ways to automate existing processes</li><li>Appointing a trusted partner</li><li>Working with large corporate organisations</li><li>Speaking opportunities at corporate events</li></ul>	<ul><li>Supporting the homeless</li><li>Working with local charities to adopt social prescribing</li><li>Effective sign-posting to people in need of a helping hand</li><li>Supporting Loneliness.</li></ul>

Marketing and Lead Generation

Market Research and Target Market

According to www.universalcoachingsystems.com To be 100% happy with your life and the path you are on, you need to be happy with the choices you are making and the results you are getting in each of the 8 life areas.

- Career and business
- Finance and wealth
- Friends and family
- Fun, recreation and entertainment
- Health and fitness
- Love life
- Personal, spiritual development
- Physical environment

The-increasing-demand-for-life-coaches is simply down to the hectic and busy lifestyles that many of us now have. More of the population are seeking out a life coach to help with one of the 8 life areas. According to the www.theguardian.com this has led to over 100,000 life coaches in the UK.

Our target customers are individuals who are capable and competent and typically want to oversee their own lives. They will be open minded, willing to listen and open to possibilities and opportunities.

They may be in transition, feeling overwhelmed, a job change, approaching retirement or searching for a university / graduating. They may be facing hardship such as a divorce or financial difficulties or simply struggling to see a way forward on their own.

Relationships are as important in business as they are in our personal lives. RELATIONSHIP-driven LEADERS focus on people, not power. They empower others and consider empathy essential to creating strong, productive teams. Many of our clients will be in corporate environments. Using relationships to enhance our leaders will develop better teams and performance.

There are allot of different requirements for coaching services, Michelle has defined 3 target groups as outlined below with some examples:

	Example Clients
Life-restructure (managing change)	- Starting or ending relationships
- Emigrating
- Mid-life crisis
- Retirement
- Menopause
- University / Graduating
Corporate	- looking for career progression – writing CV, interview preparation
- Redundancy
- Executive life coaching
Lifestyle improvement- Relationships and quality of life	- Managing Ill health
- Self-esteem needs
- Relationship difficulties / Managing friendships
- Dealing with financial hardship or bankruptcy
- Dealing with Crime
- Self-improvement
- Loneliness / Happiness

Loneliness will be a key feature within our business model and included within our strapline. Michelle will focus on loneliness; a key selling point and we will be actively involved locally in projects that support loneliness such as: campaigntoendloneliness.org.

According to psychologytoday.com there are 7 types of loneliness:

New-situation loneliness. You've moved to a new city where you don't know anyone, or you've started a new job, or you've started at a school full of unfamiliar faces. You're lonely.

I'm-different loneliness. You're in a place that's not unfamiliar, but you feel different from other people in an important way that makes you feel isolated. Maybe everyone loves doing outdoor activities, but you don't — or vice versa.

No-sweetheart loneliness. Even if you have lots of family and friends, you feel lonely because you don't have the intimate attachment of a romantic partner. Or maybe you have a partner, but you don't feel a deep connection to that person.

No-animal loneliness. Many people have a deep need to connect with animals. If this describes you, you're sustained by these relationships in a way that human relationships don't replace.

No-time-for-me loneliness. Sometimes you're surrounded by people who seem friendly enough, but they don't want to make the jump from friendly to friends. Maybe they're too busy with their own lives, or they have lots of friends already.

Untrustworthy-friends loneliness. Sometimes, you get in a situation where you begin to doubt whether your friends are truly well-intentioned, kind, and helpful. Your "friends" with people but don't quite trust them.

Quiet-presence loneliness. Sometimes, you may feel lonely because you miss having someone else's quiet presence. You may have an active social circle at work, or have plenty of friends and family, but you miss having someone to hang out with at home.

Marketing Strategy

The effective use of technology will make the business streamlined and efficient. The website will be outsourced but maintained by Michelle Heart Life Coaching Ltd. Michelle will have easy access to all areas to make amendments as and when needed. The website is responsive meaning it is fully accessible on PC, laptop, tablet and mobile platforms.

The principle objective of our business over the first 12-months will be to gain a foothold in Portsmouth and the surrounding area. We will develop and perfect our services to ensure we have a credible offer and the ability to meet the needs of our clients. We will have transparent pricing and innovative packages enabling customers to secure sessions in advance.

With these principles in mind, the following targeted programmes of work will be initiated under six headings:

Digital marketing is the marketing of services using digital technologies. The industry is lucrative and global with hundreds of specialist companies offering services. The industry has particularly grown in the last 5 to 10 years. Freelance options are available through a number of websites including www.peopleperhour.com and www.freelancer.co.uk. These are cheaper and often with similar technical solutions. The right freelancer can be just as effective and offer a good return on investment.

Our chosen freelance professional / partner will focus on the following areas:

- Search marketing
- Social marketing
- Pay per click management
- Banner advertising
- Improved conversion rates

- E-mail direct marketing

Michelle Heart will team up with a digital organisation or freelancer. We will undergo a robust selection process to ensure the "best fit" for our business. They will work to our "terms of engagement."

E-Mail direct marketing is the act of sending a commercial message to a wide group. Email marketing works best when customers are targeted and considered relevant for our market. We will create a database of customers and potential customers. We may include a newsletter or simple effective email messaging. Our databases will be fed with information from:

- All forms of social media
- Questionnaires
- Existing customers
- Connections at events

Social Media will be used to market our services and our company. Presence across the social media spectrum will include Facebook, Twitter and LinkedIn. LinkedIn is particularly important for clients looking for career development and interview preparation.

Facebook Marketing. There will be innovative content and an exciting user experience with a responsive and consistent message (posts – likes, share and comments). Users are updated with new and engaging service offers using videos and colour to drive traffic to our website.

According to statista.com the number of Facebook users in the UK is 39.2m and this figure is expected to grow to 42.2m by 2022. The figures represent accounts that get used monthly and do not account for dormant users:

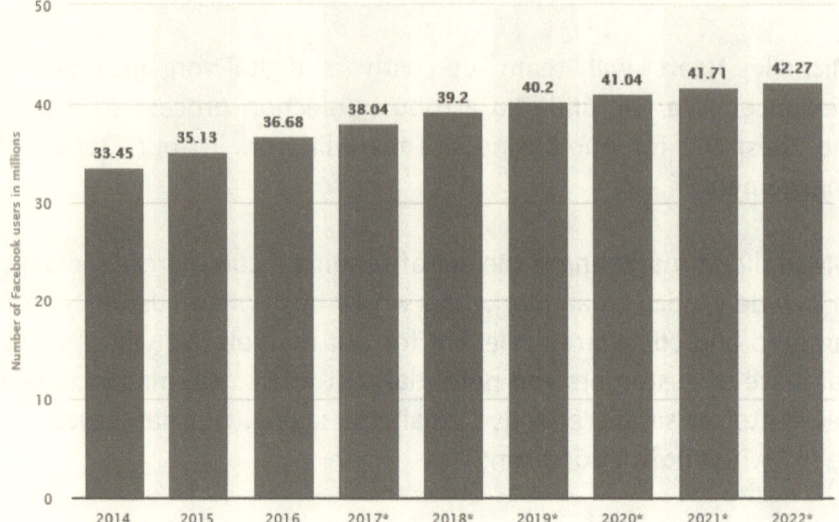

Twitter marketing. There will be interesting content, engaging user experience, responsive and consistent message (hash tags, following and tweets /re-tweets). Users are updated with new and engaging tweets about our services and offers to drive traffic to our website. Once a tweet reaches a certain level and size (number of users), the message will be used to reach a wider audience.

LinkedIn marketing. LinkedIn is the biggest social network site dedicated to business with around 20 million users in the UK. Effective use of the platform will include:

- Build an industry network both online and in person.
- Gain new customers through on-line recommendations and word of mouth.
- Keep an eye on our competition.

Affiliates and Partnerships. Thinking about our target market, Michelle has created a strategy for developing partnerships with organisations who have an over reaching arm to our customer base. We will approach all partnerships, following a simple strategy incorporating the following key elements:

- Identify the decision maker within an organisation.
- Use a variety of different communication tools, including emails/direct mail followed up with a call a couple of days later.
- Direct/targeted marketing is likely to be cheaper and more effective than indirect marketing. Customers still like to receive physical materials to look at and make their mind up in their own time without feeling pressured.
- Most decision makers will run purchases through another department, either their finance department or gain final approval at senior operations meeting. This may take time on their part. Persistence (without harassing) is key.

	Target Companies
Life-restructure – (managing change)	counselling-directory.org.uk citizensadvice.org.uk www.relate.org.uk
Corporate	acas.org.uk https://www.recruiter.co.uk/directory wikipedia.org/wiki/List_Of universities experian.co.uk
Lifestyle improvement- Relationships and quality of life - happiness	lifestyle.org www.lux-review.com

Michelle heart Life Coaching will engage with all major organisations. Working to a pre-written negotiation strategy, care will be given to communicate the quality of our service. Some partnerships may turn into customers, particularly if companies are planning major organisational restructures.

Networking events. The key benefits of these event are to network with peers and spend valuable face-to-face time with potential customers. Events can be found at:

- http://www.greatbritishbusinessshow.co.uk/
- https://www.exhibitions.co.uk/find-an-event
- https://www.eventbrite.co.uk/

Michelle will review the online schedules periodically and create an event diary. Attendance will either be through purchasing a stand or attendance to gain ideas. Event marketing can be an efficient and cost-effective way to increase brand awareness and gain customers. A short strategy document will be prepared in advance to ensure key people are seen and time is effective. Events will be targeted to fit with our target market; including corporate, lifestyle improvement or people looking to restructure their life.

Customer referrals. Providing a good customer experience is the best and cheapest way to enhance our brand and maintain our customer base (customer retentions). In a highly technical world, word of mouth is still a very credible marketing strategy. Customer referrals will work best when our clients feel a connection. Providing a good customer service and client outcome will keep our customers loyal and want to tell their friends.

Awards. Nothing sells a business better than recognition. An award will provide further opportunities and give our marketing initiatives greater impact. The business will specifically target an appropriate award and dedicate specific time and resources to win. Our focus will be on coaching awards based in the UK:

- https://www.the-coaching-academy.com/awards/winners.asp
- https://www.ukcoaching.org/auth/login?returnurl=%2fabout%2four-awards

Campaigns. Loneliness has become an increasing problem in today's fast pace and an area of work close to Michelle's heart. Michelle will use her existing networks at Citizens Advice and her local involvement in campaigns with a single goal. To end loneliness. We have developed a campaign strategy that will partner with other organisations for maximum impact. The campaign has been designed to actively seek out and help lonely individuals.

Competitor Analysis

Competitors

According to lifecoach-directory.org.uk there are 16 life coaches providing services within 15 miles of Portsmouth. Most coaches will work as freelancers and have a variety of qualifications and expertise, we have listed three below:

Emma Block – Waterlooville PO7 – I'm a personal and business coach with 23 years' experience. I help people maximise their potential, live their values and create a compelling future. We will deal with the key issues as well as it being relaxed and enjoyable. Free introductory session.

Peter Black – Petersfield Hampshire GU31 – As an Air Traffic Controller at Southampton airport I found transitioning into being a working parent very challenging. I was expecting guilt for leaving my son at Nursery overwhelm from trying to do it all and stress at not being able too.

Michelle Summer – Southampton SO31 – My purpose is to help you be at your best, and experience more courage, confidence, self-belief, energy and fun in your career and personal life. You may not feel anywhere near that "enlightened" state now.

Company Structure

Team Structure

The business will run under the directorship of Michelle Heart who will remain accountable and oversee all the business duties. Specialist tasks will be outsourced, and some activities may be carried out in partnership with a specialist company, such as marketing.

The key tasks will include the delivery and supply of life coaching consultancy services. Michelle has developed a marketing strategy to grow the business, focusing on key areas including direct marketing and brand awareness. The table below sets out the business activities by task:

Activity	Director	Personal Assistant	Advisor	Outsourced
Bookkeeping	✓ 1st year only	✓		
Accounting				✓
Legal				✓
Administration	✓ 1st year only	✓		
Marketing and lead generation	✓	✓	✓	✓
Marketing events	✓	✓		
Branding	✓		✓	✓
Diary scheduling	✓	✓		

Activity	Director	Personal Assistant	Advisor	Outsourced
Online sales and enquiries	✓	✓		
Website updates		✓		
Proof reading	✓	✓		
Corporate governance	✓		✓	

After 6-12 months our business is expected to expand. We will have perfected our service model and be looking to recruit administration staff to help our business grow. We have budgeted for a personal assistant for:

- 3 days per week (after 1 year)
- 5 days per week (after 2 years)

Directors

Michelle Heart founder and director – Michelle has enjoyed a career working for a successful health and beauty retailer for the last 10 years. After achieving her Advanced Diploma in Counselling, Michelle progressed to head of HR covering a workforce of 400 staff. In 2017 Michelle completed her training in transformational coaching – Level 5 and began working voluntary for the Citizens Advice.

Jayne Smith adviser – Jayne is a serial entrepreneur having run her own accountancy firm for the past 10 years. Jayne has been friends with Michelle since high school and is very trusted. Jayne's business is successful and employs a workforce of six across two branches.

Premises

The registered trading address for Michelle Heart Life Coaching Ltd is 15 Orchid Gardens, Portsmouth. Michelle has a fully functioning home office and will hire office space locally when needed to support her personal assistant.

Most consultations will occur in client's homes or a comfortable environment at the choice of the client. Hired premises may also be used as necessary.

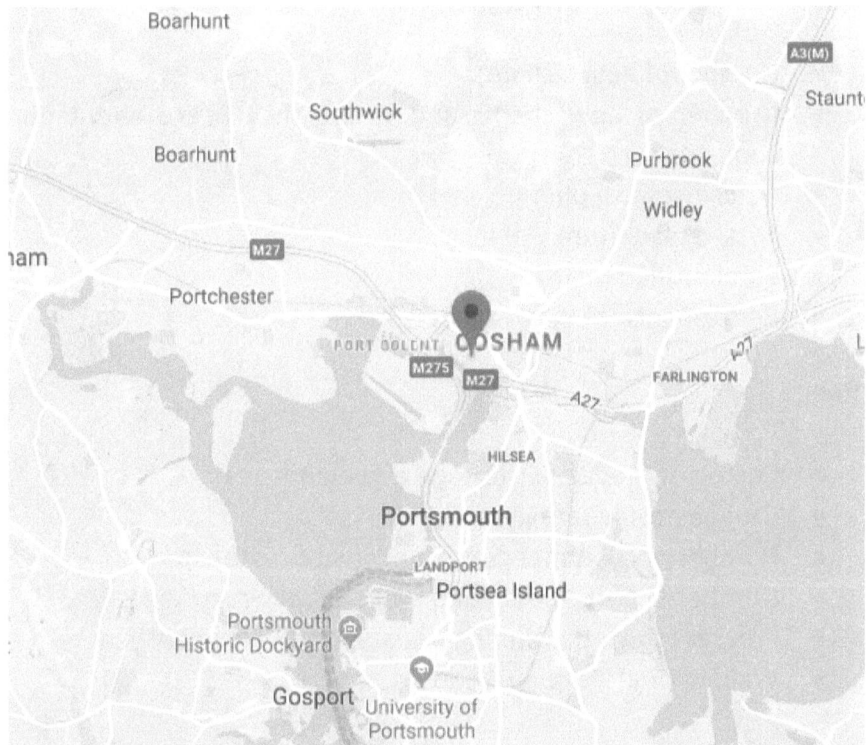

Company goals and objectives

Every month the director will review the company's financial performance through a set of indicators. These key performance indicators (KPI's) will be introduced to monitor against the business plan. Changes will be made as necessary to take advantage of good performance and address any issues.

This will include but not limited to:

Sales

- Total chargeable hours v plan
- Packages sold v plan
- Average chargeable hour value v plan
- Number of clients completing their course of life coaching sessions
- Number of active clients
- Number of new clients and where they heard about our company
- Total income v plan
- Total expenditure v plan
- Total profit v plan
- Performance of marketing events

Quality

- Customer feedback (through questionnaires)
- On-line profile rating
- Number of customer complaints (with reasons)
- Number of customers not completing their packages
- Progress towards winning a coaching award every year
- Waiting times for new clients

The data will be analysed monthly and will form an important element to the success of the business. There are three principle reasons for this.

- To provide assurance to the director that the company is achieving the sales and profit outlined in the business plan.

- To provide assurance that all packages and content is delivered and meets or exceeds clients' needs.
- To provide assurance that future lead generation initiatives are targeted in areas to generate the greatest return on investment (ROI) and return on directors' time.

The first year will focus on "building the brand" and increasing the number clients. The business will react to the performance indicators and consider the various drivers and leavers available to the company. Soft intelligence including feedback will be reviewed, focusing on the company's objectives. An understanding of what our clients want leading to effective outcomes will be the key to our success.

SWOT Analysis

Michelle has created a SWOT analysis based on her experience as an executive. The business will review the SWOT periodically to ensure that opportunities are realised, and risks identified:

SWOT Analysis Table

Strengths	Weaknesses
Director has a proven track record; Michelle has 10 years' experience as an HR executive and is a fully qualified transformational coach	Sales patterns difficult to predict, particularly in the first year
Open and transparent pricing structure	Low marketing budget
Low company overheads	
Growing market sector	
Significant networks within the industry	
Opportunities	**Threats**
Branching to other cities across the UK	Poor customer feedback
Inspirational speaking	
Increasing our margin over time	
Self- help products and/or apps	
Working with large corporate businesses	
Use of telephone and email coaching	

Financial Analysis

Start-up summary

The business requires an initial investment of £10,000 which the director has put into the company as a loan. This investment is enough to start the business and gain a foothold within Portsmouth and the surrounding area.

Michelle Heart Life Coaching Ltd will be self-funded with the initial investment used to develop the business infrastructure. This will include our website, system development, branding, secure premises and implement our marketing strategy. The business is expected to make a small profit in the first 2 years with initial revenue to be reinvested. The director can complete most of the on-line start-up activities although some tasks will be outsourced, such as website development:

Item	Start-up
Computer (laptop) +broadband	£900
Website development	£1,500
Sundry expenses	£500
Contingency	£7,100
Total	£10,000

Key assumptions

Details of all sales activity, expenditure, cash-flow and profit and loss have been provided in the financial appendix. The table below shows a summary of how the financials are expected to look over the first 3 years of trading:

	Year 1	Year 2	Year 3	Total
Sales	£39,735	£78,840	£93,420	£211,995
Cost of sales	**-£1,987**	**-£3,942**	**-£4,671**	**-£10,600**
Gross profit	£37,748	£74,898	£88,749	£201,395
Gross Margin	95%	95%	95%	
Overheads	-£28,900	-£56,535	-£66,638	-£152,073
Net profit	£8,848	£18,363	£22,111	£49,322
Net Margin	22.3%	23.3%	23.7%	

Michelle will keep the businesses financial performance in constant review. The cash-flow of the business will be an important element. Particularly during the start-up year and reviewed monthly.

The sales forecast has been created using several realistic assumptions. The assumptions focus on the number of chargeable hours. For the first 3 years, Michelle Heart will be the sole consultant charging between £50 - £75 per hour supported by a personal assistant.

Assumptions include

- Reduced income in the early years to allow our marketing strategy to become effective and iron out any difficulties that may arise.
- Chargeable hours sold in year 1 are expected to be 129 increasing to 639 in year 3.
- Chargeable hour rates will remain consistent within our packages for the first 3 years.
- Michelle Heart Life Coaching Ltd will launch will individual coaching sessions and 3 packages:
    - £75 per each 1hr session
    - £65 per hr with each Moon package (3 sessions)

- - £55 per hr with each Earth package (6 sessions)
  - £50 per hr with each Sun package (12 sessions)
- In year 2 we will employ a personal assistant for 3 days per week, increasing to 5 days per week in year 3.
- A 5% budget has been applied to any bad debts and disputes.
- Office space will be paid for on a pay-as-you-go basis with a local office provider such as: www.regus.co.uk.
- Our advertising budget will be c5% of turnover.

The primary objectives of the business in the next 3 years is to develop a credible life coach consultancy business specialising in:

1. Lifestyle improvement (relationships and quality of life – happiness.)
2. Life-restructuring (managing change.)
3. Corporate development.

www.ingramcontent.com/pod-product-compliance
Lightning Source LLC
Chambersburg PA
CBHW030014190526
45157CB00016B/2707